95559

HQ
769
.S6

Spann, Owen

Your child? I
thought it was my
child

# Your Child? I Thought It Was My Child!

# Your Child? I Thought It Was My Child!

Owen & Nancie Spann

*Ward Ritchie Press* ○ *Pasadena, California*

A dedication to: *David, Richard, and Ellen Spann*
*Christian, Peter, and Ashley Anderson*

Without whom this book would never have had to be written, and without whom we could be living in abject splendor.

An apology to: *Ashley Anderson—*
from Nancie Spann

During my preoccupation with co-authoring this book, Ashley found I had less and less time for her. She summed up her feelings one day when she marched into my room, where I was typing away madly, to state, "I don't want a writer for a mother. I want my mommy back."

She was six.

# Acknowledgments

For us, writing a book was a metamorphosis. We went through more stages than the Viking I missile headed for Mars.

During the first phase, we yelled a lot. Each of us was fighting for his own material, not really trusting the other's judgment. But as we sparred, we conducted interviews and gathered information. We are indebted to psychiatrists Ernest Pecci and Donald Lunde and writer Edmond Addeo for contributing their expertise. We also want to thank Polly Bergen for her delightful frankness, Barbara Kendall for her school tales, Walter Winter for his unique thoughts on divorce, and Thea Snyder Lowry for her loving viewpoints.

Phase II was a standoff. We didn't yell as much, and we began to discover how valuable our male/female roles were. We appreciated attorney Arden Weinberg's ideas at this point in time, along with those of psychiatrists Noel Morrell and Robert Wald. Brenda Maddox gave us insight; Helen and Frank Beardsley gave us hope; and Jeanie and Charles M. Schulz made us laugh.

Phases III, IV, and V were better still. We finally realized that we not only enjoyed living together, we enjoyed working together. We started to inspire one another with consistency and actually had fun writing.

All along the route, we found closet stepparents and stepchildren who opened up to us with surprising directness. To them, we are grateful.

Our families, too, deserve a mention: for putting up with us, for putting us down, for putting it over on us, and for putting it all into place.

Then there was Bob Howland who may have been the only one who thought we had anything in the beginning. And Bill Chleboun, who may have been the only one who thought we had anything in the end. And Joyce Janson who tried. And Lois Bird who said: "Write it." And Dr. Richard Kunin who said: "You *are* experts." And Dr. Lendon Smith, "The Children's Doctor," who actually believes in children and to whom we would entrust all six of ours.

*If he would only take them.*

# Foreword

*by Lendon Smith, M.D.*

I have always maintained that people should have fun in their lives and feel that life is an interesting challenge and/or there is yet hope ahead. One should be able to laugh a little bit more than cry. However, prevailing ethic lays heavy guilt on parents without partners; the assumption is made automatically that someone has done something wrong. *SIN* is implied. This book is beautifully dangerous in that it contends that people do not have to feel guilty or angry and that children's lives aren't necessarily ruined because their parents split up. It is also suggested that with honesty, love, and a sense of humor, two groups of people can move in together and, despite a variety of unfamiliar sights, sounds, smells, behaviors and life-styles, grow into maturity with great joy.

The danger in this book is the suggestion to those parents who feel trapped in impossible marriages that there is an easy way out; maybe by taking the plunge, a frustrated parent may find divorce and remarriage a way to reduce his/her Valium dose. Owen and Nancie feel that divorce and remarriage is not a sin but a natural evolvement of a personality growth to maturity.

Owen and Nancie begin this book after their respective divorces; they found they were partnerless parents. Their attraction, marriage, and resolution of myriad new problems are outlined in a lively, dialogue style interrupted by supportive and timely quotes from a variety of experts that Owen was able to tap because they were guests on his radio talk show. The book is surprisingly linear despite the can-of-worms nature of the subject.

I have the feeling that the hurdles—financial, physical, emotional, and intellectual—have put these two people in a situation of crisis that cemented their relationship. If young couples getting married today for the first time had to go through what the Spann-Anderson protagonists did, there would be fewer mismatched marriages ending in divorce.

The danger then is that you may like the book, try to follow its guidelines, find you are not Owen and Nancie, and feel cheated and want your money back. They have presented an honest approach to the steprelation situation in which they are involved, plus descriptions from many other persons and their comments. The multitude of interactions evolving from a re-marriage with children are too numerous to cover in a single book, however, much of the value that comes from this one is from its bright and dedicated authors. These two special people could pull off just about anything they set out to do. They tell us of many encounters with each other, the children, and ex-spouses that demonstrate their ability to communicate in ways that help them to get what they want. They both have a good self-image and this allows them to bolster each other's egos when they slip. The title suggests this feeling: they are able to love just about anything that moves and has depen-dency needs. (It is said, "To be a father one need not sire a biological offspring. One can be a sensitive friend to a child.") They admit they don't like everyone, but *that* takes a good sense of self also.

The joy of the book is the reaffirmation of the validity of some old truisms: everyone must feel worthwhile in order to maintain a good self-image; love and honesty will conquer all; give a child rules to live by but options within these rules. The authors developed these concepts because of the crisis situa-tion; these values crystallized rather quickly. But every human being living with another human being knows—or should know—the value of these human attributes.

My personal reaction to this evolving human drama is "Wow, I hope I don't have to go through all *that* to find some happiness." But maybe one doesn't know what joy is until he or she has suffered.

# Contents

# Your Child? I Thought It Was My Child!

# The Blended Family

"California is America tomorrow," proclaimed Curt Gentry as he talked about our "late, great state."

And he was right. Whatever the topics of discussion might be today in New York, Omaha, or Atlanta, chances are they are already old hat to us West Coasters.

Think back over the past decade and a half.

What other state was the first to bring you: campus riots with the ever-popular Mario Savio, beatniks, hippies, and the drug culture of the Haight-Ashbury?

What other state has brought you: surfers, Bill Graham and the folk-rock sound, psychedelic art, communal living, Patty Hearst, Charles Manson, a young Governor who sleeps on the floor, and a Junior Senator who sleeps on the job?

What other state was the first to bring you: Richard M. Nixon?

What other state has popularized the notion of today's nuclear family and, along with it, a staggering divorce rate of one out of every two couples?

Isn't it likely then, that now California should proudly present America's *next* phenomenon — *the stepchild?*

Of course, California didn't exactly invent the stepchild. That goes back centuries — before Cinderella. But we're doing

1

our best to popularize it. It's now Mama Bear, Papa Bear, and Baby Bear by a former marriage.

"When the American dream goes awry, Californians feel it first," says historian Kevin Starr. "We have the most volatile culture in the United States."

"Californians are searching for new values, new ways of living. These values may not appeal to the rest of the country today but they may well lead the way to mid-America's thinking tomorrow."

All right, you may ask, What's the big deal about step-parenthood? Isn't that strictly for the other guy?

Not when you consider today's staggering divorce figures of a million people a year. With 80 percent of that group remarrying, the conclusion is that there are a lot of kids in this country living with a nonbiological parent.

As each new marital bond is formed, someone's natural child becomes someone else's stepchild. In 1970 eight million kids were stepchildren. That's one out of seven. Now, in the mid 1970s that statistic has grown to one in six. And by 1980, based on current divorce and remarriage projections, *one child in every four* will be a stepchild.

But, California has beat America to the punch again. That one in four figure has *already* been reached in several counties of the Golden State.

One in four. A far cry from the time when Cinderella found herself in such a unique position.

Today the unique has become the norm. Yet few people talk about how it's happening. How these kids *become* stepkids.

It begins with many of these one million people a year wandering around looking for a permanent warming ground for their cold, divorced feet. Most of them do not come alone. They come as a "package" — a package filled with bright-eyed, adorable children, brought into the world to create a family that no longer exists.

In our still guilt-ridden society, we tend to avoid talking about the ups and downs of mixing broods or breeds, as it were. In fact sometimes we even try to ignore that problems exist at all, pretending the children are natural issues of the present marriage. It's not easy admitting that we made a mistake (if that's what it was) or admitting that kids can cramp our style and get in the way when we're trying to act like newlyweds.

Honestly now, as a parent/stepparent, do you find yourself vacationing at Disneyland en masse (his and hers) while longing to fly off to a romantic tryst in Acapulco?

Have you noticed those glamorous evenings spent dining and dancing reluctantly being replaced with hamburgers for the gang at McDonald's?

Or that night at the latest art flick turning into a double dose of disaster films on Saturday afternoon with the mob?

Well, join the club. These scenes can be disappointing and devastating, or they can be fun. They can scare the hell out of you or they can actually bring your relationship and your life into better focus. It's up to you.

In writing this book we simply want to share with you what we have learned and are still learning as parents/stepparents of six children who ranged in age from four to 21 when our relationship began. You will also see attitudes change from chapter to chapter as our relationship matures and the children grow.

We are not "experts." The Masters and Johnson of step-parenthood we are not, suggesting foolproof techniques that will enable you to raise perfect stepchildren. But we are sincere in wanting to help parents examine and deal with their situation with honesty, humor, and common sense. We're not going to use pretentious dialogue or fashionable terms per se. We're not going to intellectualize. What we are going to do is be practical and come up with suggestions from experience, not from charts and graphs.

**Owen:**   *Over the years as a radio and TV talk show host, I have interviewed many of the real authorities on children: Doctors Lee Salk, Lendon Smith, and Benjamin Spock, among others—all formidable people with rather impressive credentials.*

*Nancie and I together have observed and talked with those divorced parents, stepparents, and stepchildren who have moved in and out of our lives.*

*And sometimes information came to us from the most unlikely sources. When I mentioned to my two engineers at KGO that we were doing a book on stepparenthood, both of them volunteered that they, too, were stepchildren. And their two stories could hardly be considered the norm.*

> **Carl:**   My mother left my father when I was two and married another man for a few years. Then she left him and married his son. So I had two step-fathers: the original number two husband and later his son, who was my same age.
>
> **Owen:**   Was this confusing to you? Did it screw up your life?
>
> **Carl:**   Do I look screwed up? No, I don't think so. My mother died years ago, and now the only family I have left is my second stepfather.
>
> **Owen:**   Do you still see him?
>
> **Carl:**   Oh, sure, he's my kids' grandfather, and when we go down to Bakersfield, we see Grandpa.
>
> **Owen:**   And he plays the part of Grandpa?
>
> **Carl:**   No, he doesn't *play* the part. He *is* Grandpa.

**Owen:**   *Roger's story was even stranger.*

> **Roger:**   Picture this. A small town in South Dakota. My father ran the local diner and employed a woman to help him serve. They became

friendly, so friendly that my Dad and the woman talked my mother and her husband into switching mates and families.

But before anything became legal, the town busybody blew the whistle. Suddenly the cops came out, arrested both husbands, and took all six of us kids (three from each family) to an orphanage for a few days.

Finally, that got squared away. And both my mother and the other lady took their youngest children to Reno, stayed in the same hotel together, and got simultaneous divorces.

Then both newly created families left this small town. (We really *had* to leave) and I grew up with my Dad, his new wife, and her two daughters. Actually, everything worked out fine eventually, and both readjusted families are still together today.

So we gathered our information wherever we could.

We met with probation officers assigned to custody and stepparent adoptions.

We talked to attorneys about the legal aspects of adoptions and how our court system adds to postmarital difficulties. We spoke with educators from the nursery school to the high school levels.

We consulted psychiatrists and psychologists who see some of the problems arising from stepparenthood: stepsibling rivalries between "his and hers," resentments passed on by the natural mother to the stepmother, child manipulation of one or both households.

Most of the therapists were able to help us because they are living what we are: they too are stepparents.

Some of the professionals we talked to asked to remain anonymous and preferred not to be quoted. Why? Because they feel there are still too many unknown factors in the field of stepparenthood.

Government agencies? Forget them, really. We contacted the Department of Health, Education, and Welfare, the Census Bureau, the Center for the Study of Public Policy—the list was endless. They are all involved with marital disruption and the child but have not progressed beyond the area of divorce and remarriage in their research. Yet they all agree there is a serious need for information on the stepparent relationship.

So we looked for a Masters and Johnson in the field of "package marriages," but we discovered no one.

So we found ourselves on our own, sharing with you the information we have gathered over the years as well as our on-the-job experience as supportive parents/stepparents to our mixed bag of half a dozen.

We would like to try to reassure you that you are not alone. Your problems have been our problems, and with some faith and know-how you *can* live happily ever after—most of the time.

Although we are addressing ourselves to the divorced parent who remarries, what we say is generally applicable to the widowed parent, the nonparent who marries into parenthood, and to divorced people either hoping to remarry one day or who regard stepparenting as the remotest of possibilities. Beware—it can sneak up on you, and a soupçon of insight into the pros and cons may help ease a future transition.

When one considers that within a few years 25 percent of American children may find themselves with a "step" label, it opens one's eyes to the fact that it's an area that should indeed be explored.

The fact is, *the children we bring into this world are not necessarily the children we will raise to adulthood.*

Households are becoming medleys of mankind as we blend our broods and learn to communicate with feelings, not labels.

Cinderella should be among us taking her rightful place.

# The Settling-In Stage, or Instant Shock

**Nancie:** *Owen, my three children, and I moved in together on a Saturday.*

*Monday morning the children trudged off to school in a strange community. I started to unpack the 5,732 items that would turn our barren house into a livable home, and Owen began a new broadcast schedule.*

*Instead of being on the air on his old 1:00 to 4:00 P.M. talk show, ABC decided to switch him to news from 5:00 A.M. to 9:00 A.M.*

*The ratings went sky high but our enthusiasm slumped.*

*We were getting up at four in the morning, napping at mid-afternoon, and retiring early. Thanks to Daylight Savings Time, the children were going to bed later than we were.*

*Try to explain **that** to children who are expecting a surrogate parent in shining armor, not in red-checked pajamas behind closed doors.*

*I had the additional potential problem of my brood's misbehaving and looking bad in Owen's eyes.*

*Normally, one doesn't have to justify these unfortunate moments to the biological father, as the children are partly his creations too. The new man, however, is more objective, lamenting the absence of his own offspring, and not at all ready to accept or overlook your children's offenses.*

*The noises, the constant interruptions, the responsibilities— these things can be unnerving to any of us. But to one seeking some "honeymooning," it can be depressing. It's a wonder to me how any woman with children gets a marriage proposal.*

*The three most important things I tried to remember in getting through this phase—and it is a phase if it's handled right—were (1) to see my children realistically, not as the perfect creatures I wanted them to be but as the flawed, normal kids they were. In this way I could relate to Owen's annoyance with them. Although he showed patience, there was a limit. Frankly, I consider us fortunate to have had him keep us all in line. I could have become an indulgent, tiresome mother excusing their hang-ups with "they've been through so much." As it was, I couldn't overlook their faults nor could they. Owen set the rules by which we lived—and are still living happily and comfortably. We really like ourselves, and each other because of it.*

**Owen:**   *Sure, I set the rules because, without them, instant chaos!*

*I had lived the comparatively peaceful life of a bachelor for a year. Suddenly, I reinherited: fighting for the bathroom, having no hot water to shave with, and being a phone-answering service for moppets. Believe me, all this can quickly dampen any newlywed's enthusiasm for what should be rightfully his peace!*

*Let me make one other point at the risk of being hung in effigy by the National Organization for Women. A step-marriage is not for women's-libbers. In most cases it's the man who's out there fighting for a couple of bucks every day. When he comes home at night to his new instant family, he does not want the day's battles to continue. He wants peace and quiet.*

*And it's damn well the woman's job to provide this serenity. Sure, she may have had "quite a day" dealing with new resentments from ex-spouses and both sets of kids. But it's her responsibility, plain and simple.*

**Nancie:** *Back to my three points. (2) I kept quiet. I tried never to defend an action by any of my children if Owen disapproved. I respected his wishes; I did not try to manipulate him.*

*Many times I disagreed but I said nothing. After all, my gang and I outnumbered him four to one and it was important for him to become active among us.*

*With time and a home that was shifted from straw, to wood, to brick I see things differently now. My viewpoints do not always coincide with Owens. We are two separate entities with a right to think for ourselves. My children also have rights: one, to be defended by their only blood tie at home—ME. Of course I try to be cautious and not to misuse the privilege but I do feel that parents—step or otherwise—can disagree in front of kids as long as it isn't destructive disagreement. There's a vast difference between undermining a spouse and exchanging ideas with love and respect. To my way of thinking that's a* **living,** *realistic atmosphere in which to prepare children for the adult world.*

*During our fourth year together I began to do this. Not long ago Owen and I were, let us say, in disparity over the proper punishment my son Peter deserved for a misdemeanor. My older boy, Chris and my daughter, Ashley listened seriously, then agreed with Owen! That's how far we've come.*

*From the beginning I knew Owen was tough. I knew he guarded his privacy and was not a "born" parent. I knew he wasn't going to be a companion to my children. And I admired him because he admitted his limitations. He did not make promises he couldn't keep. I also knew he was sensitive, extremely kind, and had a great sense of humor.*

*One afternoon when Ashley was around four and a half, she went out walking with us. She was tripping over rocks, twigs, mounds of earth, butterfly wings—who knows what—until Owen could stand it no longer. He called her a klutz. She didn't say anything. He asked her if she knew what a klutz was. "Certainly," she replied. "That's what my brother has on the bottom of his football shoes."*

*Owen laughed so hard he didn't notice her tripping after that.*

*Without laughter, we might not have been able to get through our adjustment period. That's why, I believe, it is essential to discover who each of us is before we get too involved again and consider remarriage.*

*Do we share similar goals? Do we have the same patterns of communication? A very dear friend Richard Kunin, a psychiatrist, taught me to ask those questions. I will be forever grateful.*

**Owen:**    *Another word here from the "loyal opposition." To quote Nancie, I am not a "born" parent. I am not a "constant companion" to her children. But how many stepfathers are? Or, for that matter, how many natural fathers are?*

*Dr. Ernest Pecci, an Oakland, California, psychiatrist, says: "The average man does not know how to love children. Mother love is developed, but the average man does not know how to love children. He can take them to a ballgame, all right, but right afterwards, it's 'Okay, Mommy, you take them back.'"*

*Where do you learn fatherhood? A father has never given birth to a child. Where can you find a study course in the "role" of the man in today's society.*

*What's the answer? We try. We learn. We feel.*

*And we do the best we can.*

**Nancie:**   *Doing the best we can brings me to (3) in my personal guide to success among the step-savages: Laugh at the
absurdity of that horrendous moment when your child does
something "terrible."*

*Perhaps he has called you a five-letter word or, if he is more
imaginative, a twelve-letter word, and is in a complete rage.
Your man reacts by sending him to his room and cutting off
all weekend privileges. Now there's silence. You don't know
what to say. The child's temper is a reflection on you and
that's embarrassing. You want your new mate to think you're
terrific and your kid just blew your cover. Instead of directing
your own anger into the already tense atmosphere, getting
mad at both of them, try to laugh at yourself. Admit you're a
human being with faults of your own.*

*Explore the reasons for your child's behavior and ask your
husband's advice. Don't leave your mate out now, or he may
start to feel guilty for what he has done. Laugh at yourself,
and congratulate him. Then both of you should talk to the
child, again with some humor. The punishment speaks for
itself. You don't have to act like jailers.*

*There are far more serious dilemmas, of course, but they
may stem from small incidents like this, multiplied by
misunderstanding and lack of communication or caring.*

*Don't strip the child of his ability to see the funny side of his
behavior. He needs to understand his inner self, but laborious
delving may bore him.*

*Sometimes Snoopy and his friends tell us as much about
who we are as Freud ever did.*

In a way, the early days of stepparenthood can be likened to TV.

A television series is usually given 13 weeks in which to
attract an audience large enough to make it a winner. If it
doesn't succeed in that time, it is often canceled.

Unfortunately, many of us apply this ridiculous formula of instant success or failure to our personal lives.

Thirteen weeks is hardly enough time for anything significant to develop, except maybe weeds. And yet we have discovered from talking with court psychiatrists that many marriages involving stepchildren are failing in the first few months. Not 13 weeks, perhaps, but close.

Marriage number one has a 60 percent chance of success with most of the stress appearing in the first year—the time *without* children.

A subsequent marriage *involving* children has a lesser chance of success. Although the syndrome is under study, there are no statistics available yet to show us just how bad off we are.

The hell with the statistics anyway. The stepmarriage is turning into a serious social problem that we've got to recognize and do something about. We've got to stop looking at life through our television sets and get down to the reality of this problem. That means using our intelligence to conquer that tender emotional structure of ours, and build some character. It takes strength to be a stepparent.

As necessary as the courting period is before remarriage, it is generally an unrealistic look at what's ahead. The couple has spent time with each other's children, but only under ideal circumstances. *He* takes *hers* to the ballgame. *She* takes *his* to the theater. *They* get dressed up to go out to dinner. It's all role playing. The adult male is being Paul Perfect; the children are putting their best Buster Browns forward, and the mother is keeping her fingers crossed.

Then the marriage, and immediate chaos follows.

**Owen:**   *The following encounter took place (on the morning talk show I am back doing) with attorney Arden Weinberg,*

*psychologist and family therapist Thea Snyder Lowry, myself,*
*and, an unidentified caller, whom we shall call Jerry.*

**Jerry:**    I think those famous stepparents, the Beardsleys, are a myth. I have custody of my five kids,
and my wife has her four. And we tried putting
them together and just couldn't do it.

**Owen:**    What went wrong?

**Jerry:**    Everything. First of all, she moved into *my*
house. That was the first problem. We thought
we had it all worked out beforehand. We
talked it over with the kids before everybody
moved in. "Neat," they all said. But when it
actually happened, nothing but trouble. Like,
when one kid went to share another's bedroom — all the little conflicts added up and
became worse and worse. We couldn't handle
the constant bickering of all the kids. We had
to split. Now I still live in the house; she lives
somewhere else. Yet we love each other and see
each other — but quietly over at her apartment.

**Owen:**    Did you and your wife get a divorce?

**Jerry:**    No, we don't want a divorce, but we can't live
together either.

**Arden:**    I think I'd have to agree that the Beardsleys
are a myth, in a way. There are difficulties
in bringing up your own children, and it's
hardly the movie or TV version of the ideal
family. When you add to this, *another* family
coming from a different place with different
values and additional sibling rivalries, you just
know you're going to have problems. So why
didn't you seek help right at the beginning,

before you got to the point where splitting seemed to be the only answer?

**Jerry:** Counseling help? We *ran* for help, as quickly as we could. But it didn't work. We just had to get apart fast, before it got too bad. You see, we only lived together for four months. And what really happened is that the kids controlled us. That may sound farfetched. Here are two adults who couldn't control nine kids. But they really had the upper hand.

**Thea:** Jerry, do you want to keep talking about *your* house? What about starting over again on neutral ground, since two households are now being maintained? Why not get a big old house that needs fixing up and make that a community project so that peoples' minds are on *accomplishing* something rather than destroying something?

**Owen:** *And on and on it went. Instant Shock brought to life.*

From that very first live-in day, you can expect a lot of questions and irritations to arise. Should the new family dine together, depriving the honeymooners of their one chance to communicate alone? Can the stepdad assign household tasks to the older children? And if he does, will one of them run to phone his real dad to bitch about the weird monster who is living with his mother, exaggerating the whole story?

There may be the disruptive phone calls from the ex-wife shrieking about the late alimony check, and "let me talk to *my* children," or from the ex-husband making excuses for the late child-support check and wanting to talk to *his* children.

These phone calls invariably come at mealtime. Ex-wives and ex-husbands always seem to know when you're eating.

Some former mates have difficulty adjusting to the re-marriage of their previous spouse and find clever and creative ways to irritate and disrupt.

If you let them, they win and you lose. So don't let them get to you. Be stronger and more mature and, above all, keep your sense of humor.

Take the phone off the hook at mealtime if that's their game. Be fair but be firm—firm when they make their demands.

As far as your homelife and the children are concerned, remember what the late Moss Hart said: "It's your house and your're bigger than they are." Stepparents, don't be afraid to be *parents*.

If you want to have a romantic dinner alone, pick a night and do it. Let the children choose how they will dine that night, too. Take a tray to their room? Have a friend over? Cook their own food?

The evening meal is an extremely important social occasion for a family and should be looked forward to by everybody. It keeps us in touch with each other. Taking a night off from the routine, however, is not going to destroy its value.

In our house we compromise. We have dinner with the children, exchanging ideas and thoughts, and then have a "quiet hour" directly afterward. We stay in the dining room for coffee and candlelight; the children go off to do homework or have baths.

When coffee and candlelight turn into the urge for sex, you may find yourself with another challenge to conquer.

Foreplay may quickly become "pastplay" with a house full of kids (1) asking for help with their homework, or to be read a story; (2) falling down and skinning their whole bodies; (3) beating up on each other. Children intuitively know when to pull (1), (2), or (3), and it's always when you're having S-E-X.

File this irritation along with ex-wives and ex-husbands phoning at mealtime. Deal with it the same way. Taking the phone off the hook won't help, but you can take your brain off the hook for a while. Nine times out of ten, the children will survive their crises without you, probably caring for themselves and each other pretty well. That's teaching self-reliance, isn't it? So stop feeling guilty. And enjoy.

Besides, if you make the mistake of waiting until they are asleep, you may miss *your* chance, because somehow they always manage to outlast you.

So how should *you* handle *your* experiences during this period of adjustment?

**Nancie:**    *With patience.*

**Owen:**    *Liquor's quicker.*

# Finding That New Love Mate With a Big Heart

**Nancie:** *If you haven't found that love mate with a big heart yet, what's the rush?*

*Get the patterns from the last marriage out of your system first. It's a lot easier on everyone later on. Take your time because one cop-out leads to another. Having played it safe, hanging onto a bad marriage for convenience, may lull you into running away from responsibility again. And stepparenting, as great as it can be, is a responsibility.*

*However, today is today. Congratulate yourself for being where you are now. And mean it. Don't wallow in the fantasies of the past, remembering the good times. If you really counted them you'd probably find they were damn few.*

*Take my word for it. Your good times are ahead.*

*There is a transition period, however, that is not at all pleasant. Think of it as going through withdrawal pains. But once you've kicked the habit of that former marriage, there is only one way to go—up!*

*The divorced male, if he does not have custody of the children, gains an immediate and fuller freedom than the woman. He sees his children on Saturdays or Sundays, but for*

17

*the rest of the week his time is his own to do, date, or dream as he wishes.*

*Many men actually go through their "stewardess phase," priding themselves on the youth and number of their conquests.*

*But finally the time comes when that nesting instinct returns to the old bird along with the realization that he'd better pick on someone his own age.*

*At this stage the Lothario may find himself back in his original social circle, dating the ex-wives of ex-friends. But they can turn out to be kookier than the kook he just crossed swords with in court.*

*When the dates include his children—as a sort of get-acquainted period—he soon learns which women are genuinely interested in him as a "family man" and which aren't.*

*Those enormous hazel eyes may have Daddy spellbound, but they can't con the kids.*

*If you're a divorcee how can you start a new life when you've got the issues from the old one staring you in the face? Your children are looking for stability, and you are about as stable as Jello. You're overwhelmed by your position. You're feeling resentful and hemmed in. You may even question why you ever had children. Psychologists will all agree **that is** a very natural kind of ambivalence.*

*So get a job.*

*Child support is essential.*

*Alimony is demoralizing.*

*Quit raving to your friends on the phone about what a bastard he is and start some self-evaluation. If you need to rehash hurts, go into your bedroom and talk to yourself. Even with a therapist you have to come up with the compromises and solutions yourself, and this way is cheaper. It really works. So talk to yourself, but,*

*Get a job.*

*Get out of the house. Be with people who treat you like a new experience. They don't care who you were; they want to know who you are. And don't say there is nothing you can do. You've been doing a lot of things for your family all these years that you take for granted but which have value.*

*Go to work in a pet store. God knows, you've cleaned up after enough of them.*

*Work in a children's shop. You certainly know about clothing children's bodies.*

*Or work in a kitchen boutique. You may not have been Julia Child but you must have picked up some expertise among the pots and pans.*

*Hire yourself out as a hostess's helper. What hostess, the day of a dinner party, isn't desperate for another pair of skilled hands? By that time she'll be glad to pay someone to arrange flowers, polish last-minute silver, bathe and feed the children. You were there once, too.*

*Beneath you? Really? Isn't cashing those alimony checks beneath you?*

*Go work in a bookstore. You always kept up with the latest novels and discussed them pretty well at parties.*

*You see? There are things you know you don't know you know. It's not easy, but you can do it, and you're going to like yourself.*

*Sure, you need a sitter and that's the hard part. Don't tell me. I've been there.*

*For seven months I took my children to a sitter's house at 6:00 A.M. five days a week because she was all I could find.*

*I had a welfare mother and her child live in for a while until she left us for her lover.*

*Then there was the older woman. Ideal? Unfortunately, not. I came home from work one day to find my seven-year-old son and his friend Oliver dueling with kitchen knives. My ideal surrogate mother was standing there terrified, biting her knuckles. I yelled "Cool it," and that was that.*

*The boys looked for pillows to sit on for a few hours, and I looked for another sitter.*

*I had a young lady who slept all day and an unwed pregnant teenager who needed psychiatric care.*

*One girl tried to sue me for $25,000.*

*No, it wasn't easy, but the children and I survived until still another option came along and, in the meantime, I was making a little money.*

*True, most of it went to child care, but the effort made me feel like a responsible person, not just an alimony check-casher, or a divorcee looking for a meal ticket.*

*The best way to find a new husband, if you're looking for one, is not to look for one.*

*Shedding one mate for another without an interim period of learning to depend on your own resources is neurotic and could get you into more trouble with your next liaison.*

*Sure, you're desperately lonely and frightened, and the children need a man around the house. You can rationalize a million ways. But you are not facing the real problem: making yourself strong enough so you'll never be that dependent again. Marriage should never come from need. Marriage should come from want.*

*At this point, you don't know what you want. You only think you do.*

*Don't look at every man who comes into your life as a prospective husband. Look at him as a possible friend. That kind of relationship takes time to cultivate, so relax and make friends instead of your next wedding dress.*

*The ultimate relationship is when friends become lovers, and lovers become man and wife.*

*But before you can get to that stage, you've got to learn about each other.*

*Get to know each other's bad habits. Find out what he likes to eat. You may have to drop Mexican and learn to cook*

*Italian. Develop interests together. Determine whether or not your goals are similar. Do you enjoy the same way of life? If you're a night person, find an owl. If day is for you, get yourself an early riser.*

*Don't try to solve problems that you think you **might** have. You'll draw them to you. Be realistic about what is happening now.*

*And have fun together.*

*During this period of developing friendships, the children will be uppermost in your mind.*

*"Will they be confused if strange men come to the house to pick me up for a date, or should I meet the men elsewhere?"*

*Would you like it if your children didn't think enough of you to bring home their friends for you to meet? Do you limit the number of friends they can have?*

*Children are people too, and they need to be treated with respect and common sense. If you view your dates as friends, not potential stepfathers, your youngsters will not feel threatened. They will be delighted to see a smile on your face again. After all, they benefit from your good moods.*

**Important:** *Always have the sitter at your house when your date arrives. It is not his obligation to reorganize his travel route to pick her up for your convenience.*

*Always pay for the sitter. The children are yours. The expense is yours.*

*For the first few dates with the same man, take the sitter home yourself. If you want to invite him in, suggest he mix himself a nightcap while you drive her down the block. It pays to find someone close by.*

*Later on, he will probably offer to take her home while you make coffee or slip into something more comfortable. (We'll get into **that** in the next chapter.)*

*Wait until he offers, though, and be sure to pay the sitter in front of him so he doesn't think it's his obligation when he drops her off. He'll really appreciate your consideration and respect your independence.*

**One tip:** *If the date is a dud and you never want to see him again, move fast. Help the sitter on with her coat, press the money into her hand and ask, directly, if he would mind taking the girl home, sweeping the two of them out the door before he knows what hit him.*

*Be sure to say thank you for the lovely evening.*

# Your House 🏠 or Mine?

**Nancie:**   *Generally the problem is the woman's—how to get away from the children for the night.*

*Be definite. "I'll be gone overnight, but I'll be back in time to fix breakfast. Mrs. so-and-so sitter will stay with you. And there's chocolate cake for dessert. You'd be amazed how often chocolate cake smooths over departures.*

*That's mature mating.*

*How about frenzied fornication?*

*He comes in for that nightcap. You go check on the children and just happen to remove all those tight undergarments.*

*The first thing you know is the next thing you know: you want to get laid.*

*Making love is a privilege you shouldn't turn down as long as you take responsibility for it. Be discreet, however. Do another bed check of the children and walk to your room with a certain decorum. Lock the door. Coitus interruptus is not recommended. Then enjoy. And sleep. Sleeping alone after making love is like serving caviar without champagne.*

*If the kids beat the alarm clock, emerge from your room explaining that the reason for the locked door was that you wanted a little privacy. Enough said.*

*On the weekend use your ingenuity. Send them off on an errand—for money, of course. You're not above bribery at a time like this. Get them out of the house, if only as far as the back yard. If your friend gets caught sneaking out the front door, he can always be **arriving** to take the entire bunch to brunch or the beach.*

*Naturally, making a habit of this is unwise. Your luck won't hold out forever, nor will you feel good about yourself or the relationship.*

*As much as you would like to believe that the **real** Prince Charming is out there anxiously waiting to sweep you off your size six double A's, it really isn't so.*

*Be cautious. You are extremely vulnerable after a divorce or widowhood, and what fills the vacuum temporarily may not be what you and your children need permanently.*

*This goes for the lonely man as well. He may be trying to replace his missing family.*

*Both of you are playing around with too many lives to be a Lost-and-Found Bureau.*

*So, although you need warmth and sex, don't consider it love to justify enjoying it. Keep the children out of your fantasy of remarrying until you are sure you even like each other. If you don't take time now, you'll find yourself looking for another lawyer later on.*

*This experimental period is easier to handle when the children are older and you have good communication. New York psychiatrist Dr. Lee Salk says, "As children become more knowledgeable, sexual matters will take on the right meaning. Children, then, will be better able to tolerate parental affairs."*

*He goes on to say that with children in the three- or four-year-old category it's tougher. Changing sexual partners can be disconcerting. They get the idea that the parents' relationships are not stable, and they prepare themselves for separations. Their expectation in life is that relationships don't last, and that people are not to be trusted.*

*So it's important to work out your sleeping arrangements so that you get what you need without compromising your little one's psyche or your self-respect.*

*Sometimes a lady's reputation takes a beating regardless. At least, that's what happened to me.*

*While the children and I were still living in the house that was community property, my former husband felt it was his right to keep and use the key whenever he chose. I could have had the lock changed, of course, but I was working too hard for the small amount of money I was earning to spend it on something nonessential. And besides, it seemed like picking lint.*

*However, it was an infringement of my privacy, as I found out one Sunday morning. Just as I was about to get into the shower, the doorbell rang insistently, forcing me to lunge for a robe and tear down the stairs. Still mostly naked, I reached the landing in time to watch the front door open before me.*

*The father of my children and I stared at each other in total disbelief.*

*I then turned to call upstairs. "No, no, Ralph. Stay where you are."*

*At that point I remember nothing specific, only a series of serious words directed toward me and, I think, my morals. Then something about the children. I managed to spurt out that they were with my mother for the weekend before the door slammed. I never did get to explain about Ralph.*

*I was dog-sitting for a friend.*

*During the dating game, the most common meeting place will probably be the man's apartment. If he too is divorced, the apartment will probably be tiny and sparsely furnished in "early Goodwill" but don't knock it. That apartment offers both of you the most relaxed atmosphere you'll find anywhere under the circumstances. You'll find that candlelight and Gallo can enliven a multitude of spaghetti dinners, as well as Colonel Sanders and pizza and ribs from the nearby deli.*

*Lobster, escargot and Lafitte Rothschild are forgotten treats, since the woman is broke paying the all-night sitter, and he's broke paying everybody.*

*If both of you have children living with you, another alternative is a motel. Needless to say, that can be costly unless one of you owns it.*

*Furrowing in a friend's flat is fun, but fabulous friends are few.*

*Going on vacations together is constructive. It gives you uninterrupted hours with which to be bored with each other— or joyously contented. Discovering this early is very important because if you do marry, those little people grow up and one day you will find yourselves alone. You had better like it.*

*Leaving for a trip with a love partner will not destroy your children's respect for either one of you. As long as they don't see you in bed together, they're not going to put much thought into your sleeping arrangements away from home.*

*That's what you can expect from them, and that's what they can expect from you. After all, you're human, and that's why they love you.*

# So You Want To Be a Stepparent— or Do You?

Taking on the responsibility of becoming a stepparent can be frightening, and it should be. If you aren't frightened, you may not be taking the situation seriously enough.

On the other hand, you can't be *too* frightened, or you may shy away and possibly miss enough experiences to write a book of your own!

You've got to remember that life is one big boogeyman. If it all turns out right, you're a hero. If it doesn't, the fickle finger is pointed. Because you've got a 50-50 chance in either case, you might as well take control of your destiny and feel good about yourself.

A good start into stepparenting is to stop battling your windmills for a while and concentrate on the fears of your children.

Kids can be bewildered and frightened when a remarriage is imminent. Look what they've been through—the divorce of their parents and the shattering of their whole world. Often the kids feel guilty and responsible for that marital failure.

They also feel something else — fear for their own self-survival. One psychiatrist told us, "What I hear from these children is: 'Who's going to feed me? Who's going to take care of me?'"

Dad has left the home for good. Then Mom leaves one day to get back in the job market, or just to start dating, and the children become anxious that she too will never return.

Then another trauma. One parent or the other comes along with a semi-stranger who is about to move in on their territory, and they feel threatened again. They don't want to be hurt any more than we do. And secretly they're still hoping for a miracle to bring the original family back together.

But your decision has been made, and you ask yourself, "How do I tell my children I'm getting married again?" Or, more likely, "How do *we* tell *both* sets of children?"

Don't tell them anything. *Ask* them.

Just as a young swain asked his prospective father-in-law for the lady's hand, why not have the future stepdad make points with his stepchildren-to-be by asking for their mother's hand?

The thought of a 45-year-old man confronting an unsmiling teenager with braces on his teeth, or a preadolescent with a runny nose, or a wide-eyed nymphet clutching a teddy bear, or any combination thereof, might seem absurd at first: "Uh, hi there. I'm your friendly, neighborhood stepdad type and I would like to ask for your mother's hand in marriage." But then where's your sense of humor? As a matter of fact, if you don't have one, you're in a lot of trouble right off the bat because you're going to need one. As we've said, it's an essential piece of equipment in the stepparent game.

In dealing with your own children, take them out to a meal (special treat time), and explain what you want to do, asking their advice. It's important to be candid with your kids during the courtship. If you're honest with them and respect their intelligence, they'll be more apt to treat you the same way when you ask for their approval. But if you've played games with them, resorted to devious explanations, and hidden your true feelings while you've been dating, you'll probably get from them what you gave.

A generation ago, many of our parents played games with us. Subjects like death, illness, and divorce were just whispers behind a closed door. This only gave vent to our imaginations creating a worse situation than actually existed. It was wrong then, and it's wrong now. Be open with the kids about this new family union.

If they give you reasons they don't want you to remarry, listen carefully to their objections, but be firm. Don't let them manipulate you because, as we will point out later, *a child's manipulation can be the single most destructive force to this new marriage of yours.*

Be understanding of their position. But your final recourse is neither giving in nor buying them off. It's your life. See that *you* live it. Just make sure you know what you're doing.

Make sure you know the real reasons for wanting to remarry.

Dr. Ernest Pecci sums it up this way: "Too many times a woman remarries simply to find someone to take care of her kids. She is saying to the man, 'I'll marry you. You'll take care of me and my children. My ex-husband won't be able to get them away from me. I'm going to marry you and prove that my ex-husband was wrong because I'm going to have a perfect marriage with you. My kids are going to love you so much that the natural father will eat his heart out.'

"Often, she will work much harder at this second marriage. She'll get all the kids involved in a conspiracy of silence . . . to play along in the lie . . . that they all love the new spouse. She wants to show that the original divorce was not her fault — that she just married a bastard. She will often choose a man who will never leave her, he loves her so much. But everyone is role playing, and no drama goes on forever. This new marriage is bound to end up in disaster. And the step-dad may end up with the kids, not the wife."

So know what you're doing in this remarriage of yours. It is supposed to involve love for both partners—not financial security for one.

It's also supposed to involve love and respect for the children. The more you *ask* them, not *tell* them, the more chance you'll have of bringing them into the fold.

There are certainly areas that concern children, and allowing them alternatives within adult limits strengthens their ability to make choices and gives them a feeling of belonging to the new and often alien household.

Perhaps they can be given a choice in school district or neighborhood or the living accommodations themselves. Kids love to house hunt. If that experience is yet to come for you, try to include them in the search. You have chosen each other. Now choose your environment together. Then they can stake a claim to *their* room and dream about how to decorate it. You're giving them an address, how about letting them identify with it?

If you *are* buying a house, the woman who has received money from her divorce (or has money of her own) should contribute as much as she can toward the down payment if her children are going to live with her and her present mate. Just as she should have assumed the obligations of paying for the sitters when she was dating, she should continue her monetary responsibilities for her offspring. Because they are sharing the home, the cost should be shared as well. The stepdad must not be expected to undertake all the financial burdens unless he is a natural undertaker. The poor man can't support his children, an ex-wife, a new wife *and* her children without sinking faster than the SS *Poseidon*.

What we're saying is that when the mother is receiving child support and the stepfather is paying it out, a practical commitment is essential to keep the household solvent.

Even when the groom is a sheik with oil up to his turban, the mother should pay for her children's expenses out of the child support checks. The need for financial security is very real when one has children to worry about, but it is rarely enough to sustain a remarriage that is not built on a more loving foundation. One shouldn't get in the habit of accepting without giving, because marrying for the wrong reasons backfires sooner or later, hurting not only the adults but the children too.

There are variables, of course, depending on who has more money and more children. It's a moral decision to be made by the couple with honesty and consideration.

We have discovered a "give-and-take" arrangement that fits our pocketbook.

**Nancie:** *I financed the down payment on our house since my three children were going to live with us. Owen agreed to cover the mortgage payments. I paid for refurbishing the house and the taxes on the property until my money ran out.*

*I receive child support with which I pay for my children's clothing, entertainment, allowances, supplies, sitters, meals out (with or without us), and their portion of vacations when we take them along. Their biological father pays for most dental and medical expenses (I pay for medicine), and when the children visit him, he deducts the cost of feeding them.*

*Household supplies and the food consumed by everyone, including Owen's children when they are with us, is my expenditure. Owen pays all the costs of running the house.*

*After that, I leave it up to him to decide what more he can do—or wants to do—without being made to feel put upon.*

*We have separate bank accounts and make our financial decisions independently although within the responsible limits of our prearranged commitments to our mutual household. Owen's money is his, and mine (as custodian for my children) is mine. We thrive with the attitude that neither is subservient to the other fiscally or emotionally.*

*A woman must not resent (even in the deepest part of her consciousness) money spent on her husband's children. She takes on that contingency when she commits herself to another parent. Buying for his does not mean buying for hers. Equality is for the races, not for stepparenthood. And what seems inequitable at the moment may not really be so if you have faith.*

*For example, when Owen and I began our alliance, he obtained the loan on the house in his name because the bank thought he was a better risk than a divorced woman. I put up the money. We were not married nor did we intend to get married. Each of us had suffered the pain of divorce, and we honestly felt we were foolish candidates for a legal liaison. But we loved each other maturely and sincerely wanted to share a family life. We felt we could create a wholesome atmosphere for the children by exposing them to a loving home, and that seemed a lot wiser than exposing them to a bad marriage or a fitful, unfulfilled mother.*

*We pooled our resources and moved to suburbia, bric-a-brac to bicycles. The neighbors didn't know what to make of us. There was a Mrs. Anderson with three crazy children. Then there was Owen Spann coming and going. ("You know him — from radio and television.") It finally dawned on the block that his coming and going wasn't visiting—he was live-in help.*

*There were phone calls and deliveries for a "Mr. Anderson" and a "Mrs. Spann." The postman eventually gave up and left anything with our address on it in the mailbox.*

*My former husband agreed to our arrangement reluctantly. I assured him in a document that no matter what happened to my relationship with Owen, he would never have to contribute to my support. That turned the tide. One can't blame any man for wanting to get off the financial hook.*

*My children accepted our decision without complaint, although it wasn't ideal for them. Explaining the family tree at school put them on the spot, and one child was worried that the police might come to arrest us.*

*But Owen and I did not assume the guilt of what a bad influence we were on the children, nor did we allow the morality of our Victorian backgrounds to force our middle-aged minds into something we weren't ready for. Instead of fretting, we spent our time meshing our neuroses, having fun, and loving a lot.*

*Our life became such a joy that one night at dinner Owen said, "I think I should propose." With control I never thought I had, I said, "Propose what?"*

*We were married two weeks later.*

The ceremony took place in a fierce rain storm on the island of Hawaii. The church was Congregational; the minister, Asian. He seemed inexperienced — or perhaps it was that we were *too* experienced. In any event we pressed on with wet feet, an improvised ring, and two witnesses we had never seen before, and we had the most touching wedding and wedding day one could hope for.

That one was for us. But because ours is a stepmarriage we felt we had to do more. Expose our merged families to the merger, as it were.

If you've been through it or are planning it, you may already know that it isn't easy to get custody of every stray sibbling for a "his and her" wedding.

Stepchildren can be hostile (or be committed to the hostility of the custodial parent), be out of town, be away at college, or even be babes-in-arms. They can come with variegated dispositions, in all sizes, from anywhere, and they are *not* always available when you want them.

But we decided not to settle for disappointment. We decided to keep trying until we got it right.

So we get married every year. We get married on our anniversary, and whatever family we have with us joins in. Besides the emotional rejuvenation of renewing our vows and picking up our option on each other for another twelve months, there is a peripheral benefit of planning any kind of ritual we want, drawing on the availability, the imagination, and the skills of the children.

Psychiatrists say children should not be included in the ceremony to the point of making a commitment to the marriage, nor should a boy be asked to give his mother away as it is too heavy a responsibility for him and the connotation is unhealthy. There are, however, many constructive ways to get them wholesomely involved. They can bake the cake, concoct the punch, string flower leis, or play their instruments. Who needs an organist when you've got a budding bagpiper?

Adding an original prayer to the service mentioning the children and welcoming them to the new family seems like a nice idea, too.

Because there are no legal or religious restrictions to an already married couple, it's only a question of proclivity and imagination.

Besides the Asian minister, so far, we've been married by a rabbi, a Catholic priest, and an Episcopal clergyman.

Next year we plan to find a sheriff and have a shotgun wedding.

# What Do We Call Each Other?

The wicked old stepmother. The drunken stepfather. The deprived stepchildren, crying softly in their beds. In fairy tales "step" is an ugly, negative word.

According to famed San Francisco etymologist Peter Tamony, the origin of the word "step" is no better than our fairy tale recollections. It came into use in eighth-century England, where it first appeared as "steop," referring to an orphaned or underprivileged child. First "steop child," then "steop-mother" and "steop-father." That's a hell of a way to start a relationship.

The French handle the problem in a most beautiful way. They call a stepparent "beautiful parent." *Belle-mere. Beau-pere.* The children are called *belle-fille* and *beau-fils.*

In Spanish, it's expressed with an ending: *stro, stra. Madrastra. Padastro. Hijastra. Hijastro.* Not bad.

But the Yiddish is a bit disappointing: *Shtiff-mutter. Shtiff-futter.* Oy.

All European languages have a word for "step," but there is no equivalent that we could find in the Polynesian culture nor among primitive African tribes.

It seems that in some areas where survival was the primary concern, the difference was never established in the language.

With early death such a common occurrence, the remaining families simply took care of the survivors without distinction. Illegitimacy was treated the same way. A child was a child. A parent, a parent. Period.

It was only in Western society that the relationship began to take on qualifications. It was important to know who was who.

The more civilized we became, the more we discriminated. And look where it's gotten us.

It has been our goal as stepparents to eliminate these antiquated implications and get back to loving, not labeling. How can we expect to live happily ever after if we're huddling in divided camps?

In our family we play a game. We have dropped the word "step" from our vocabulary completely. We now test our word power by substituting more imaginative adjectives. And the challenge may appear when you least expect it.

We were having dinner at a Chinese restaurant one night with five of our six children. Sitting at a round table in the center of the room we were, naturally, drawing a lot of stares. Secretly, we were basking in the glory of parenthood. For once, the group was well behaved with no one needing a haircut or a clean shirt.

Then came something we weren't prepared for. A friend came to the table to say hello. Although he knew we had recently married, he had never met the children.

Introductions!

We solved the problem by saying: "We'd like you to meet *our* children: David and Ellen Spann—Christian, Peter, and Ashley Anderson." Each child kept his identity without losing status in the new family arrangement. It was assuring, yet accurate. It was a spontaneous reaction that worked for us, and we have continued to use it whenever appropriate.

That's the key. Discovering appropriate and warm ways in which to show respect for the natural parent without destroying the security of the child.

To us, maintaining respect for this absent parent is important. For that reason, we have never encouraged the children to call us either "Mommy" or "Daddy" in the step-parent role.

When Ashley, the youngest, was five, she wanted to use "Daddy." We explained to her that she already had a Daddy, but we gave her an alternative. She could choose a nickname that would be hers alone. Actually, we fell into that easily because while we were living together *Mister* Spann became a gag nickname that all three Anderson kids used. After a while, however, the boys decided, "We can't call you *mister* forever." So, they settled for "O." Ashley chose "Owie," a wincable sobriquet but her way of getting close. The Spann boys, already young adults, had no conflict. Ellen, considerably younger and from a different mother, opted for "Nance." Problem solved.

Of course, we were aware of five-year-old Ashley's need to be reassured of her position with her stepfather by calling him "Daddy," but we didn't feel her psyche would be seriously affected by facing the question honestly. If psychiatrists tell us that children can accept truth more easily than adults, why not be honest?

We had two other factors to consider: Ashley's real father, who lived close by, and her stepsister, who lived across the country and whose visits were limited to school vacations.

Naturally, we wanted to make Ellen's visits as happy as possible. At eight, she was feeling understandable resentments about her role in her father's current household. We didn't want to compound her confusion, if we could avoid it, by having her endure the ultimate slap in the face of hearing a brat from left field call *her* father "Daddy."

Ashley's father had the same understandable resentments. He did not want to be replaced. He was assuming his parental obligations and, therefore, insisted on keeping his title on an exclusive basis. We feel the natural parent should be allowed to retain his dignity, even if it might be considered ego gratification.

There is controversy on this point. Most psychiatrists say the child should be allowed to call both fathers "Daddy" to reinforce the parental role within the household. But from our experience, it seems the child can relate to having two fathers much more easily than the two fathers can accept sharing their position. So we're dealing with what's comfortable for the adults, not what's best for the child.

But doesn't truth and logic have value in these relationships? The truth and the logic of the situation is that the stepfather is not the child's real father so why pretend he is, unless the biological father does not care to assume the part? We may be wrong, but we chose truth. Only time will tell.

As a matter of fact, Ashley put together the truth and logic theory quite accurately in a social situation not too long after that.

**Nancie:**   *Owen and I were visiting at a school open house when Ashley told us that her teacher's helper was a fan of Owen's and wanted to meet him. She took us over to the girl and said, "This is Owen." She hesitated a minute, gestured toward me, then added, "and this is Nancie." (If stepdaddy is called Owen, then Mommy is called by her first name too, because the roles are equal in her eyes.) We assured her that her resolution was acceptable, and the three of us shared a healthy laugh.*

*But in all fairness to those who disagree with our decision, Ashley, later, did show signs of difficulty that I feel were related to this decision.*

*During second grade, teary, emotional outbursts at school became more and more frequent along with her stories of how she was adopted. She and I talked out her whole biological background—even Chris and Peter tried to reassure her that she had, indeed, been born into the Anderson family. Yet it persisted. Eventually Ashley's teacher strongly suggested I take her to see a psychologist. I decided to try again to get through to the problem and, believe me, I was winging it.*

*"Honey," I said, "You're very mad at me, aren't you, because your dad and I don't live together any more?"*

*She who is never without a long answer to the shortest question said, "Yes." I hit pay dirt.*

*"You're very mad at Owen because he's not your daddy. Right?" "Yes."*

*"You're very mad at your dad because he doesn't see you enough?" "Yes."*

*"Ashley, let mommy tell you something. You have every reason to be very mad at all of us. We have changed your life in a way you don't like and I don't blame you a bit for being angry. Being angry with us is all right."*

*My young, vulnerable daughter looked at me with a relief that could have been felt by a stoic and so far there have been no new outbursts nor tales of the adoption of Ashley Erin Anderson.*

*I doubt that she and Owen will ever love each other. However, I do think that Ashley will grow up having learned a most important fact of life: One does not have to love or expect to be loved to have a worthwhile, happy relationship with a fellow human being.*

The "what do we call each other" game does not end with setbacks like this. When we think about who we are to one another, and how important we are to one another, we keep working on solutions.

Suppose the mother is out shopping with her child and her stepchild. She meets a friend she hasn't seen in years. Introduction: "I've remarried, and I'd like to present my daughter, Ashley, and my new daughter, Ellen."

In this situation don't try the last name gambit we used in the restaurant, or it could come out something like this: "I've remarried and my new name is Spann. My husband's first name is Owen. I'd like to present his daughter, Ellen, who is visiting us from New York, where she lives with her mother and stepfather. And this is Ellen's new sister, Ashley Anderson, who is my daughter from a previous marriage."

Just keep it simple.

Other mother, other father, new daughter, new son, new sister, new brother. Nicknames at home, and last names when they fit.

Our children have even combined names for the sake of our dog. She certainly belongs to all of us, so they decided to call her Daisy Spanderson. Who knows, you might get a few laughs putting your names together.

**Nancie:**   *If there is only one child in the household with a different name, I like the possibility of hyphenating his name with the stepfather's. He retains his origin while linking himself to the present family.*

See the opportunities? The game can be constructive and really good therapy. The children feel special—no longer second-rate, and their image of the steprelationship improves with each additional solution.

Erase "wicked," "drunken," and "deprived."

Fill in the blanks with loving labels.

# Discipline: Who Does What To Whom?

"Love, honor, and obey" was a promise wives of a generation ago made to their husbands-to-be. And as we think back to the lives our parents led, some men enjoyed living up to the macho image of family leadership, while others were destroyed by it. Those who were destroyed simply didn't want to be the boss and were actually resented by the women they were married to.

Today's new stepfather has all the hang-ups our fathers had, besides being totally confused about what his role *is* in this new household. What is expected of him?

In earlier days, the feeling was that if a child was born of your body it was, like your wife, *your* property, your possession. You could get away with anything, short of murder, and according to psychiatrists, sometimes with that. The moral code of the times assured you *you* were the best judge of what was best for your children.

Often today, the new stepfather does feel he must immediately exert full parental control. It is not uncommon to hear him say: "Okay, this is my house. I'm paying the mortgage. I'm buying your food and your clothes, and you'll do as I say."

And, in effect, he may *be* paying the bills. The natural father, upon learning of his ex-wife's remarriage, may feel he

41

is off the hook: "What the hell. She's found another sucker, so I can forget about those monthly checks."

The instant family, the new stepfather already knew about. The instant debts could come as a surprise.

How do children react to the stepfather who takes this hard-line approach?

For the smaller ones, bewilderment followed by resentment. According to Dr. Don Lunde, Associate Professor of Law and Psychiatry at Stanford University: "The smaller kids will go along with Mr. Tough while building up resentments that may well explode many years later. The teenagers, however, may instantly and openly rebel. They may seek out the natural parent, flee the household completely, or fight back. The child-battering syndrome of years ago is now being equalled by older childrens' physical attacks on the adult figures in the household."

So what is the new stepfather to do? Here he is, a relative stranger in his own home. Obviously, some rules of daily living have to be established. Two very different and distinct problems arise: (1) how do you establish some sort of control over young people whom you really don't know that well, and (2) do you expect your new wife to go along and agree with your decisions? Remember, she must equate her love for you with what she feels is fair and just for her children.

If the two of you can't work this out, chances are you can't work out your marriage either.

**Owen:**    *On one of my radio shows dealing with the subject of remarriage and discipline, the following call came in and laid it right on the line.*

    **Caller:**    Hi, this is Dan. I want you to know that my first marriage failed over conflicts in raising my stepchild, and it failed needlessly. My first wife had been divorced for some time and had been alone with this only child. The child was not exactly spoiled *rotten,* but she was pretty spoiled. I imposed a little discipline. I played it pretty light, but it was a situation where *any* discipline was a 100 percent change. This created a great deal of conflict between me and my wife, a conflict that just got so great, we finally separated and got a divorce.

Psychiatrist Don Lunde, a former stepfather who recently became an adoptive father, commented on Dan's call: "Dan is exercising a rather common thing that we see, often originating from the parent that the child is living with, in this case, Dan's former wife. She was feeling a sense of failure over her previous divorce, saying to herself: 'What have I done? I've let my child down.' So this parent tries to pay the child back — with material things: goodies, outings, etc. . . . instead of working on a sense of security and a sense of: 'It's okay, your world isn't falling apart.'

"We often see a child who has been given so much, yet the child doesn't understand what all this giving means. The perspective just isn't there. Then, when the new stepfather comes in and tries to assert a different kind of standard, what it means to the parent who has been raising this child is: 'Hey, you've been doing a lousy job. I know more than you do, so now it's time for me to take over.' And that's pretty destructive and frightening to the person who's been handling the situation up until then."

So the new stepfather is treading a very fine line, trying to establish rules of conduct while learning to be a father to his wife's children, all at the same time.

Actually, just being a father today is not that easy under the best of circumstances.

In his book *Men's Liberation,* encounter group leader Jack Nichols says: "In today's nuclear society, the role of the father is that of provider, period . . . . Fathers find it difficult to be friends to their children except on weekends and the major tasks of child-rearing have been left to the mother . . . . His relationship with his children [often] lacks the rapport and give and take of a cultivated, easygoing friendship . . . . He has no training for the role of parenthood. . . . The nation's courts give ample proof of the sorry state of fatherhood. They award custody, in most divorce cases, to mothers. Fathers, even though they are financially capable, are discriminated against on the grounds that mothers make better parents. The father's role — that of provider — continues even after divorce, even though the pleasures and intimacies of fatherhood are often denied."

**Owen:** *How many of us even know what these "joys of fatherhood" are? A group of newborn babies were monitored electronically for several months at home, to ascertain the interaction between baby and father. The shocking results showed that most fathers spent less than 60 seconds a day in any physical contact with the baby, holding, feeding, or just plain touching — less than 60 seconds a day.*

Yet, as that child grows, so do dad's pressures to be a pal, counselor, and disciplinarian. And he feels guilty if he can't fulfill all of these roles. And most of the time, he can't.

So, if today's male is having a hard time making it as a natural parent, what possible chance does he have as a stepparent?

If he starts out on that hard-line approach we talked about, he has no chance at all. Remember, these are children who have probably been living in a postdivorce household where there has been no male authority figure for a long time.

How then can a man enter this household, call a meeting, and lay down immediate discipline? As in Dan's case, the results could be disastrous, both for the family and the marriage.

Doesn't it make more sense to *earn* the kids' respect, rather than demand it?

Dr. Lunde has suggested this type of communication with the children: "Look, this is a tough experience for all of us, and I want you to know that I have some concern about it. Sure, I married your Mother, but I'm also interested in being a parent to you. And you're going to have to help me with that. Because I don't know you; you don't know me. Now, as we do get acquainted with each other, we're going to have some basic ground rules to start with and see how they work. So, let's all stay loose for a while and see what's best for all of us."

Suppose the new stepfather wants his new daughter to take a bath. If she rebels, say: "Look, I understand you'd rather play house, but it is getting late, and I want you to take your bath now. But may I have a kiss first?"

How about the relationship with an older child if you want him to weed the back yard? "I know you want to play baseball, but this is a big household, and we really need the cooperation of everybody." Tell him how much you'd appreciate it. Succeeding is one thing. But succeeding and making a friend at the same time is even better.

George is a business analyst, 45, who recently remarried into a household with two daughters, ages 7 and 11. We asked him about his problems establishing some household rules.

He told us: "Initially, as a stepfather, I felt guilty telling the children what to do. The natural father can relate to the kids much more easily and directly. He has the prerogative, but one of the questions in my mind was: Did *I* have that prerogative, making certain demands?

"That was a big problem in my mind. But still, I *am* the live-in father, and I feel I am required to act on their behalf to provide information or to direct them. I feel I have the answers, because I am an adult. Sure, it was a questionable situation in the beginning. It still is. Let's say, I ask them to clean up their rooms. Maybe it's a test, in which I'm asking them to do something and waiting for a response. They can is either tell me to 'shove it' or go ahead and do it. They could shout back: 'You're not my father.' I keep waiting for that line. So far, it hasn't come up, mostly because their mother has supported me in my decisions."

**Owen:**   *And therein lies the secret: the rapport between husband and wife and the necessity for backing up one another.*

*When I became stepfather to Nancie's three children, not only was I as confused as any other new stepfather, but I had three totally different personalities staring me in the face.*

*Chris, then 12, had been living the "man's life" with his natural father, where he pretty much fended for himself—fixing his own meals, washing his own clothes, cleaning the house —and spending a great deal of time alone. He moved in with us full of deep-seated resentments and a lot of hurt and anger.*

*This was my first test. And I have to admit that his anger set off my anger. My solution, right or wrong, was to ground him. I realize it's not much fun being a member of a new family while in solitary at the same time. And I'm sure that, on many occasions, Nancie held back tears of compassion for him but she kept quiet. And she did support me, right or wrong.*

**Nancie:**   *Yes, I did have some bad times over this. When I look back now, I wonder how I was able to hold my tongue.*

*I felt terribly guilty about Chris's unhappiness. His hostility with Owen and me was simply a cry for love. But, of course, how could I expect Owen to like a monster, let alone love him?*

*We had one very important thing going for us, though. We had confidence in our relationship and we never doubted that it would all work out.*

**Owen:**   *I'm sure I did overreact in the beginning, but together we did something right. Today, Chris and I are the best of friends. He has brought a D average in school up to C's and hasn't been in solitary since.*

*The two younger children adapted to our new family much more easily. Peter, then seven, was most eager to please, although, at times, I'm sure he questioned just where his loyalty should be, since he is extremely close to his father. And we've always encouraged him to maintain that closeness. My only problem with Peter today has absolutely nothing to do with discipline or his being a stepchild. He is an extremely bright student and loves to brag about his straight A's in front of the other two kids. So I have to get him to cool it publicly, while praising him privately.*

**Nancie:** *Peter really isn't any brighter than any other child. All children are bright. But each in a different way.*

*Richard, Owen's second-born son, for instance, expended no apparent effort to reap incredible academic rewards, yet his brother David plodded along the C trail. Today it would be difficult to say which of them is better educated.*

*Chris is physical, a natural athlete and good with his hands. He does not like to study or read books; but he can fathom the most complicated sheets of instructions and assemble or repair almost anything.*

*Ellen has a gift for conversation that could put William F. Buckley to shame, with confidence to match. She remembers everything she hears and is able to enter into discussions on any subject, turning the talk to include her experiences with a deftness that is fascinating to watch.*

*Ashley has a little of each. She's quick, physical, loves to read but doesn't like to study, and has a well-developed vocabulary—sometimes, too well developed.*

*Now as far as Peter goes, he has a meticulous mind. He's orderly and responsible. He loves to study. School comes easily, but in things, like sports, that don't come naturally, he works until he's mastered them. He's a perfectionist who is, currently, captain of his football team and star quarterback, vice president of his class, and an A student.*

*Peter is too serious. After school one day, he told me how he had done badly on a science test because he had been thinking about his football plays. The answers were the same he had given correctly a few days earlier on a similar test so he knew he understood them.*

*I laughed as I told the story to Owen later.*

*At dinner Owen teased Peter about it, and Peter's eyes welled up with tears. Peter thought he was a failure and, as important, he thought I had betrayed him. I was his mother, with a prior commitment to him. I had known him longer than I had known Owen and, therefore, I should not tell this "stepfather" such an embarrassing story.*

*We had to explain to Peter that we have no secrets from one another, and sharing the bad with the good is what makes a successful family. Owen pointed out that we admit our mistakes in front of him and the other children, and he must learn to admit his mistakes in front of us. The experience turned out to be a strengthening one, although hairy at first, only because Owen took a great deal of time to tell Peter that he was OK; but, I think, it shocked us both into realizing how Peter's public display of boasting was really only his need for reassurances, too.*

*So Peter no longer has to be a closet bragger.*

**Owen:**   *Nancie's daughter Ashley was nearly four when our new household was formed, and she had never known any male authority figure. I'm not sure she does yet. She is a small human being, completely surrounded by dirt, who doesn't know the meaning of the word "yes."*

*Ashley could be described as the independent blithe spirit. Her average day consists of: balancing on the tops of things as high off the ground as possible (so far she has had five black eyes), mothering and housing the small creatures of the animal kingdom, and cuddling up in my lap while I am trying to write this book.*

*I have given up on Ashley.*

*What we've learned about discipline is: there is simply no one set of rules that can be applied to all. We are dealing with children, of course, but people too, and each with feelings and personalities of their own.*

*I just hope I have been as supportive of Nancie as she has been of me when my daughter Ellen has come to our home during her vacations, although I have an idea that many things have been worked out without my ever knowing about it.*

**Nancie:** *At first I wasnt going to respond to this last paragraph but then I realized my reaction confirmed my very attitude toward Ellen in the beginning.* **Don't make waves.**

*She was with us for such short sessions we wanted to make the time happy for her. Owen wasn't about to discipline her. He just wanted to enjoy her, and I certainly didn't want to play the wicked stepparent role, so I absorbed my irritations rather than expressing them as I was accustomed to with my own children. God knows, they and I are accustomed to that.*

*Even Chris, Peter, and Ashley seemed to understand, although we never verbalized it. If Ellen got away with something they couldn't, they'd just shrug and say, "Oh, that's all right. She's not here for long."*

*But patience, finally, wore out.*

*Two summers ago I drove the four children to Lake Tahoe for a week's stay. After having made the drive, unloaded the car, put away the groceries, cooked dinner, and made up the beds, you might say my blood sugar level was low. Ellen came into me as I was scrubbing the kitchen floor and said, "Well, I guess I'm going to have to sleep on the couch in the living room. There's no other place for me." I looked up and slowly articulated, "There are four bedrooms, and eight beds in this house. Find one and get in it."*

*That night Ellen became a true member of the family.*

# Must I Love My Step Child?

Must I love my step child? Does money bring happiness? No, but it helps.

Let's face it, in any stepparenting situation the relationship is going to be easier from the outset if there is genuine love for everybody. But that's not always possible and it's simply not essential to a healthy environment if the other elements are there. Substitute consideration and respect, and you've got a good chance for a viable household.

What might be more important for us to ask ourselves is: "Can I be *fair* to this child?" Seeing a child objectively, with real insight, may be a far greater contribution to his development than loving him, as some natural parents do, through fantasies of what he is and what he should be. Overindulgence, smothering, and fantasy trips in the name of love give love a bad reputation; therefore, in being *fair* we may be giving a gift with more value than we think.

Helen Beardsley, the famous mother of eight of hers, ten of his, and two of theirs, says, "You can't love 'em all."

Another mother we talked with said she had forgotten she *wasn't* her stepchildren's real parent.

50

Both women are raising someone else's offspring happily and with success so who's to say what's right?

**Nancie:** *Each child has separate needs. I know I have had to be flexible in groping my way into an honest, comfortable place in the lives of my totally different stepchildren.*

*Ellen, for instance, has a very definite mother and stepfather who shower her with most of what the world has to offer. There is no way I can compete financially nor would I try, morally. As I see it, my role is to expose Ellen to the basics. Getting her to kick off the latest fashion in footwear to feel God's miracle of grass between her toes without worrying about splinters or the myriad of objects one can step on, has been a real achievement.*

*Ellen has a mother's love. What she needs is an earthy friend.*

*For that I can be sincerely available.*

*I adore David. I didn't know that when we first met. It wasn't instant magnetism, nothing as pat as that, but because he was already an adult, polite patience shifted into the nitty-gritty fairly fast. I swore in front of him; he swore in front of me. I yelled when I thought his ideas were crazy; he yelled when he thought my ideas were crazy. Our mutually warped sense of humor bonded our black souls. While he was in the Air Force I wrote a letter asking if I might visit him. I suggested he book me a hotel room overlooking the war. He sent word that I had a reservation at the Hanoi Hilton.*

*David's mother spent a lot of years raising him. If she's ready to retire, I'm willing to take over.*

*I don't know what emotion I have for Richard. He is an enigma. Not because either of us wants it that way; it's just a matter of opportunity. We haven't had any. He lives in Georgia. I've tried to put together the pieces of his personality that I have gleaned from various sources, but the puzzle is still incomplete. I think of him. I think of him when I am alone with my thoughts, when I don't have to think of him. I think of him as a splendid experience yet to come. After all, he's his father's son.*

*He has promised to drive out from Atlanta with his girl friend to see us, perhaps before this book is finished.*

*Yes, they will be welcome to share a room in our home, in full view of my children. I understand that this young lady is his security blanket among strangers, and my children will understand that Richard and Sally are adults as Owen and I were when we lived together.*

We all have the capacity to love. It's really a matter of choice. But do we choose to love *everybody?* Of course not. As adults there are people we love, people we like, and people with whom we simply have no rapport. We try to get along with each other, but we don't put the pressure on ourselves to fake ardor we don't feel. Not if we're realistic.

So why don't we apply the same hypothesis when dealing with stepchildren? Some are lovable and some aren't.

Forcing yourself to kiss a stepchild who gives you a pain in the ass is a sham and, more important, will be felt by the child. Even an ass has feelings, and the lesson he learns is that kissing is an obligation, not a sweet reward for caring and being cared about. Better to give a sincere hug. At least that's encouraging. And it does leave room for conversion!

And who knows? It might even happen to you.

One stepmother we interviewed told us her story.

"I can recall when I was first with my husband and his children. I kept asking myself if I would be able to make space in my heart for these children who were strangers to me. I searched within myself for the answer to that question for months. Then one weekend, we all went camping and the little boy fell down and began to cry. I just felt myself so flooded with love, it came down, ZOOM, on top of me. It really surprised me."

Writes Dr. Stuart M. Finch, in an article in the *San Francisco Chronicle,* "All children are not created equally. Each is differently endowed. Some are active. Some are passive. Some are curious, some are indifferent. Some are timid, some aggressive. We should see children's qualities not as abnormalities, only as differences."

**Nancie:** *There is a mother in Ashley's Brownie troup who has a darling, demure daughter. Recently, this young woman remarried and inherited a very active, interested, demanding six-year-old boy. I have watched her go from a serene, "got it made" way of life to complete chaos. She has become a constant criticizer of her stepson, punishing him for the slightest infraction. Utilizing Dr. Finch's theories, I just wonder why she can't stop comparing this boy to her own quiet and acceptable child, and begin coping with his personality as an individual, rather than as an undesirable alien? That way, she might be able to work through this conflict. Well, it's easy for me to say.*

These character problems and clashes appear frequently in so-called stable, unbroken homes, so think of the implications in a stepfamily where children are arriving, not only with teddy bears and tennis rackets, but with inherited traits and life-style experiences unknown to the stepparent and, possibly, to the estranged parent, too. How can we love what we don't understand, or feel threatened by?

"He's just like his mother. What can you expect?"

An angry slip of the tongue like that may imply an inability to accept a stepchild for himself, rather than seeing him as the product of a stranger, about whom we may feel insecure or resentful. The child's credentials are an accident of a gene mix. Must he be blamed and remain uncared about because of the way in which the concoction came out?

Natural parents can fall into this trap, too. The child acts as a constant reminder of the "hated" parent because of a biological resemblance. "Eyes like your father's" can be a devastating accusation instead of a loving compliment.

Sometimes it is, then, the custodial parent who cannot love his own child and, subsequently, if the remarriage ends in divorce, the stepparent may be the one to ask for custody.

Arden Weinberg, attorney and family counselor in San Mateo County, gives substance to this attitude: "This situation does occur more frequently than most people think, particularly in the event of a long marriage where the attachments are strong, or when a stepparent may just feel it is in the best interest of the children to stay with him or her."

Mrs. Weinberg also told us that in California today the court will seriously entertain the possibility that the stepparent may, indeed, be the better parent.

In Jack Nichols's book, *Men's Liberation*, it states that: "To be a father one need not sire a biological offspring. Fatherhood is being a sensitive friend to a child. . . . Men must be liberated from the idea that their fertility is a measure of manhood."

Most women have intrinsically felt this way, so it's exciting to see the focus shift for men — from machismo to meaningful. It's got to be a giant step forward in establishing more connected and emotionally attached family units within this increasing phenomenon of the stepfamily.

**Owen:**  *And men really do want to try. Sometimes they just don't know how, as I discovered from a call I received during one of my radio shows.*

*The listener explained that he had been a stepchild and now at 26 is a stepparent to an 11-year-old boy, a unique premise to begin with considering their ages are so close for a parent-child relationship. But that wasn't his reason for seeking advice from my guest of the day, Thea Snyder Lowry.*

*His name was Hank and he started by saying: "I didn't think there would be any problems with my stepson because I'm so closely related to the situation. I thought about all the things that were lacking in my stepfather so I've tried to become more involved with the boy, but I'm finding it difficult. The things I wanted as a stepson,* my *stepson doesn't care about. I bought him a baseball mitt and tried to teach him the game, but he has no interest. He doesn't want to get into scouting. He lacks motivation in everything including the piano lessons his mother and I are providing."*

*Thea's reply was right on target: "I hear a young man who's flip-flopping between his parent state and his child state. Hank, you're trying to be a good stepparent but you're not listening to your son. Put yourself in his shoes. He's in the same relationship with you that you were with your stepfather. And he's probably thinking that you're letting him down because you're not interested in what* he's *interested in."*

*Imagine, if this pattern were to go on, how it might be in about 15 years with this boy having the same conflicts with his stepchild?*

*Let's go back to Jack Nichols's quote again: "Fatherhood is being a sensitive friend to a child." If you can do that, you can offer so much more to the child than the natural parent often does. And I think that, in spite of many mistakes, I'm finally succeeding in being just that to Nancie's children.*

*This may not be the most ideal time to discuss our ten-year-old resident genius, Peter Eric Anderson or "Peter the Great" as he modestly likes to be known, because, as I am writing this, he is directly below me, in his room, having been grounded. Massive screams of protest are wafting through our heating system as I write these very words. How did all this happen, especially, since several days ago Peter's teachers told us how he was "the perfect student, considerate of others, the natural leader, and the joy of her class"?*

*This all happened, because, sometimes he is* not *all these things at home, and having been fairly warned not to continue to berate his little sister as "dumb, stupid, and a brat," he continued to do so. I hope that he will learn something, and that tomorrow we can resume our clarinet lessons together.*

*Do I love Peter the Great? Yes, I do. For the most part, he's easy to love. And I have a big built-in advantage: We like the same things, we're interested in the same things, and we spend hours talking about the same things.*

*He's a football and baseball nut. So am I. So when Alvin Dark gets fired as the manager of the A's, or when Kenny Stabler's knees are giving him fits, that's really of great concern to us both.*

*He just took up the clarinet because I had played the clarinet, so again, it's easy to help him search for the B's, C's, and D's, while wincing at every squeak.*

*Peter loves his real Dad very much and sees him frequently, but I think he also has a very warm feeling of . . . shall we call it "love"? Well, certainly respect for me.*

*If my son Richard has been an "enigma" to Nancie, I might have to use the same word here, only in a different sense. Chris, the teen-ager, is an enigma not only to me, but to his mother, and to his natural father in the sense of trying to determine the best way to deal with him. He is extremely sensitive. He has never been a good student, although we have managed to help him raise his grades somewhat. And he, himself, is torn between what he wants out of life, and how hard he wants to work to achieve it.*

*Right now, he's almost old enough to drive a car. Cars are his one overwhelming passion. He can take one apart; he can put one back together. He waxes cars. He polishes cars. He loves cars. In a few months, he keeps reminding us, he will actually drive one.*

*Yet, will he? Time and time again, we've reminded him how important his school work is this year, and that if he doesn't maintain a B average, there'll be no car at all. In California, a B average means you are insurable at lower rates. So the incentive is there. But Chris isn't. He's too busy* working *with cars and somehow believing that the B average will just suddenly appear. And it might.*

*He wants to go to the University of Colorado and learn to be an architect, so he can move to Snow Country, build A-frame chalets, and live the quiet life. But how much does he want all this? Enough to work for it?*

*Maybe the problem isn't Chris Anderson at all. Maybe it's the fact that he's almost 16, and like all boys that age, he's off into his own world. Maybe we should eliminate the middle teen years so that all children would advance from 13 to 18 automatically.*

*There's been another problem here. Unlike the relationship between Peter and me, with our common interests, Chris and I have no common interests.*

*He loves skiing, shushing down a mountain in subzero weather, with the ice forming on his eyeballs. Show me one flake of snow, and I head for the nearest bar.*

*He loves sailing: man against the winds, storms and tidal waves, the thrill of almost keeling over into the briny deep. Show me a bathtub that's too full, and I reach for the Dramamine. My idea of battling nature is to watch miniskirted secretaries on a windy day.*

*If fatherhood is "being a sensitive friend to a child," the best I can hope for with Chris is being a sensitive friend to a sensitive child.*

*He often does come to his mother and me with his problems. We do listen. We do try to understand. And we do try to help.*

*I am Chris's friend. And I think he is mine. Our home is his home. And if successs is ever measured by how many companions your son invites for dinner, we are winners.*

**Nancie:** *Invites for dinner? How about spending the night? One Saturday morning Owen discovered five boys sleeping* *on the floor in Chris's room. They'd come in late and unexpectedly from a school dance.*

*I tried to point out that it was better than finding five girls, but my little jest was met with steel emanating from those baby blue eyes I had learned to love.*

*Owen may tolerate extra teenagers at dinner but* this was too much. *I thought he was going to hit the ceiling—very possibly with one of the children!*

*It's one thing to marry into a bunch of strangers; it's quite another when the strangers begin to bring home other strangers to be faced at the breakfast table.*

*I must say, though, my husband pulled himself together and was perfectly charming over the french toast.*

*As the boys were saying their good-byes and thank yous, I even found myself replying, "Oh, anytime. There's always an extra floor."*

**Owen:** *Ashley Anderson is seven now, going on 32. And that's the truth if a kindergarten experience of hers is any indication. She was asked by the school reporter what she wanted for Christmas, to which she replied, "To sleep with Santa."*

*If I ever screwed up a stepchild relationship in the beginning, this was it. Here was this little four-year-old who had been raised by Nancie to be completely independent. Ashley had never really known a male figure in the household. So I had a chance to move right in, be super-nice, and woo the young lady's heart overnight. But I didn't.*

*Why not? Because all I saw was this small person whose voice was five decibles too loud and whose pitch was three octaves too high—a small person who used this remarkable vocal ability at any time of the day or night. I saw a miniature Ethel Merman.*

**Nancie:** *That's the breaks, when a mother brings a musician into the house.*

**Owen:** *As a newlywed, I wanted peace, and frankly, this moppet was a pain in the family room. As the youngest, she also required more of Nancie's time, and I'm sure I resented that.*

*(As I am writing this, the subject in question is peering over my shoulder, having recognized her name in print. She is also holding her pet hamster, Ginger, dangerously close to the back of my neck. "What are you writing about me?" she is asking. "You'll find out when we finish the book," I am replying. "Meanwhile please get your pet hamster Ginger away from the back of my neck.")*

*In our relationship Ashley and I have evolved from resentment to respect to feeling. How? Frankly, I don't know. Was it the strange living creatures she brings into the house? The weird little friends who peer at me in the bathroom? Or, those times when she snuggles up to me on the bed and goes to sleep on my shoulder?*

*Maybe it was none of the above. Maybe it's that friendships need time to develop. Ours took three years, but it was worth waiting for.*

**Nancie:** *The young man settled in the corner of the airport motel lobby looked like David. It could be Richard; but Richard was supposed to be a crew-cut towhead, and this boy had brown curly hair.*

*By the time I deduced that the pictures Owen had of his number two son were at least fifteen years old, the cute stranger in the jeans and modified afro approached us.*

*It was Richard, with Sally not far behind.*

*They had flown out from Atlanta the night before on the red eye special. Because their vacation turned out to be one week instead of two, driving west as they had planned was impossible. There was nothing left for Owen and me to do but send them the plane tickets and worry about paying for them later.*

*How do you meet a son at three in the morning after not having seen him in twelve years? Owen wisely decided to get them a hotel room, let them sleep, and then pick them up for a late, late breakfast.*

*At that first meal, we discovered that Richard had been just as apprehensive as his father about this long overdue reunion. Verbalizing a mutual fear was a good beginning, I thought.*

*I also thought that Sally was as aware as I of the importance of our female roles. We could bridge the gaps, give encouragement and understanding, and yet maintain a level of objectivity. I don't mean to make us sound like a couple of pioneer women loyally forging through unknown territory at the side of our brave warriors; I only suggest it was an easier transition with us around. Yet I most definitely do wish to imply that a willing stepparent of either sex can add a tremendous and obvious dimension to a meeting like this.*

*The week went fast.*

*We took them to see their Atlanta Braves beat our hapless Giants. We took them to dinner at a magnificent restaurant overlooking the world. We took them to a Chinese feast with my three children. We toured a winery and introduced them to one of California's finest grapes. We showed them Carmel, Pebble Beach, and Monterey.*

*The rest of the time they took the car and went off by themselves during the day to sight-see and visit people they knew. Then I would cook dinner, and we'd have a typical meal with open-end conversation. One night I invited a friend of theirs to join us for cracked crab, a western treat they'd never had before. In other words, we functioned like a* family.

*Predictably, Ashley fell in love with both Richard and Sally. ("I think Sally's pretty and nice. Richard is cute.") They were her grown-up family. They played with her and seemed not to mind that she wanted to be with them.*

*Chris looked up to Richard, too. "He's really nice and fun to be around. And does he look like David!"*

*Peter's face lit up with equal delight when he referred to them.*

*And so it went. Getting to know each other. Well, we did and we didn't.*

*Owen mentioned wanting to get off alone with Richard, to talk a little. Richard nodded, but it never happened. That fear again.*

*It was probably for the best, considering that it was our first encounter together. Getting close but not too close, yet.*

*Most unexpectedly I found myself alone with Richard, however. I seized the moment to let him know how much we cared about him, and that our home was always open to him and Sally. I explained that he must never think the long-imposed exile had been his father's idea. His father had loved and missed him very much all those years. It was a matter of Owen's former wife's not being secure enough within herself to handle the presence of Richard and his brother. Owen was forced to shift his loyalties to his wife and their child to keep the peace.*

*It's not easy being a parent.*

*I, too, had a painful decision to make when I sent my Chris to live with his father several months after our divorce. Chris's behavior, in his confusion and frustration over the family's breakup, was taking its toll on the two younger siblings. Peter emulated his brother's negativism. They fought constantly. Even Ashley, as small as she was, was developing cranky habits. I was working long hours, running a household, and trying to be a mother to a zoo act. Something had to change. So I sacrificed one child to save two.*

*No, parenting is not easy. The scars run deep for many of us.*

# Resentments

Hold onto your hats. Here we go.

First, let's introduce the players. You can't tell the players without a scorecard.

*Ex-Wife*
v.
*His current wife*
*Her ex-husband*
*New stepchildren*
*or her own children*

*New Wife*
v.
*Ex-husband*
*Ex-wife of current husband*
*Stepchildren*

*Ex-Husband*
v.
*Ex-wife*
*Ex-wife's new husband*
*Current wife's ex-husband*

*New Husband*
v.
*Ex-wife*
*Ex-wife's current husband*
*New stepchildren*

*Children*
v.
*Children, both natural and step*
*Both households*
*Everybody else*

"That woman is a whore. She slept with your father before they got married!"

Harsh and cruel? Of course. But, unfortunately, court probation officers admit this is not an unusual remark for a mother to make as she sends her children off to visit that "other" household.

The same effect can be accomplished in a more subtle way: "Your father is taking you *where*?" "When are your father and what's her name picking you up?" "Don't forget to tell *her* about the medicine you have to take in the morning."

**Owen:**  *Although Nancie and I are entering our fourth year of marriage, my ex-wife has* yet *to speak her name, to pronounce the word "Nancie," let alone admit she is alive.*

*During vacations, when Ellen is visiting us, my ex will place a person-to-person call to our daughter, so that she will not have to speak to anyone else.*

*I've had mail from her delivered to my office. I've had her new husband's secretary call my office about a pair of socks that somehow didn't make the return trip with Ellen.*

*You name it. We've been through the trivia.*

Actually, summer vacations can bring many resentments to the boiling point almost immediately.

A friend of ours married a man considerably older than herself and each summer they inherit his four children for a month. As the kids were about to leave their mother in New Jersey for their annual California vacation, her parting shot was: "That new marriage of your father's isn't going to last. By the time he's 60, that 'girl' will only be 40. Isn't that ridiculous? How can they live together like that?"

Resentments, downgrading, one-upmanship — all programmed into our children by parents who are hurting. And those parents have done their job well. The results are evident the moment the kids get off the plane.

**Owen:**   *On one of my radio shows involving resentments, one caller put it this way: "My husband and I have two children of our own and each summer my four stepchildren arrive from the East. I've got to admit, that is the worst month of the year for me. Those kids come ready for a fight. Over the years, I've found myself always in the position of trying to win their acceptance and, perhaps, holding in the anger and minor irritations that result when they are deliberately trying to goad me. Sometimes, you find yourself being overly strict with your own kids, your natural kids, in order to bend in favor of the stepchildren, just to avoid a fight. I realize I'm not being honest with anyone, as a stepparent or as a real parent. And I don't like myself very much for this month of 'play acting.'"*

*Psychiatrist Don Lunde answered the caller in this way: "When the stepkids arrive with blood in their eyes, tell them that you're going to treat them exactly as you treat your own children. The biggest acceptance you can ever give them is to treat them the same way; and that may mean with strictness, or it may mean with permissiveness, whatever your particular style is. You must get angry with them, be unhappy with them, punish them, or love them, exactly as you do your own. That's the way to make them feel they're a part of the household, a part of the family."*

*Educator Barbara Kendall added: "How about a dialogue once a week, sort of roundtable, where each child is given a chance to say how he feels? No holds barred. And no judgment given. Nothing is held back. Let it all hang out."*

A child's visit is an important occasion for everyone. It's a special time for the kids and the parents to really get to know each other. Isn't it a shame that these visitation periods, set aside for the family to be together, often end up as a battleground for resentments and guilt?

But where do all these problems start? Do they start with the children blaming themselves for their parents' divorce? Do the children think they were not good enough, smart enough, or nice enough and that they let their parents down in some way during the marriage? It happened to one of ours. Chris was nine at the time and said: "I thought Dad was leaving *me*, not Mom, because I didn't obey him." So simple and so damn poignant.

Or does it happen when either husband or wife physically packs up and leaves the household? Is that when inner guilt turns to open resentment?

The spouse remaining in the home, usually the wife, becomes the "injured party." "Your father left us. He doesn't love *us* anymore. I wonder if he even wants to support *us*." In some instances, this injured spouse never does assume responsibility for contributing to the deterioration of the marriage. She continues to refer to her former mate as her husband. His identity is her identity, and she refuses to let go of the image. Seeking her own place in the sun is less attractive than living as a victim, feeding off fantasy, and using the children as weapons to maintain her position.

This is happening to a neighbor of ours right now. She still refers to herself as "Mrs. John Smith." She accepts her alimony and child support checks to maintain her lifestyle, while depriving her children. She's made no effort to go to work and has declared: "I don't want to get a job." She fills her days with lessons, bridge clubs, and luncheons. She's never home when her children need her, and now her drinking is becoming a problem. When she does let the children visit their father, they arrive needing everything, from clothes and shoes to seeing the dentist. So their father ends up paying and paying and paying, which *he* resents. *She* resents his leaving her in the first place, and the *children resent being put in the middle*.

**Nancie:**  *From time to time at the supermarket I run into a fortyish divorcee who has recently remarried. Last time she cornered me between the lima beans and the tomatoes to fill me in on her current domestic hassle.*

*The ex-husband has not remarried but he's living with his secretary and her 15-year-old son. Now he wants to set up a double-dating deal with this boy and his daughter, his new paramour and himself. The mother is flipping her lid, calling her ex every name in the book, feeling her 13-year-old daughter is being rushed much too quickly into adulthood. The girl has never dated before and, all of a sudden, is thinking about this boy more than her school work.*

*On the other hand, the father feels this is the way to learn how to date. He believes it's better to learn how to deal with the opposite sex under controlled situations rather than in the back seat of a car.*

*Although the mother knows she's overreacting, she found herself saying to her daughter: "The next thing I know you'll be asking me for the pill." The daughter lashed right back with: "Mother, what kind of a girl do you think I am? Don't you trust me?"*

*The new stepfather is caught in an impossible triangle, fraught with very possible disasters.*

**Owen:**  *What is an ex-husband's role during this period of turmoil? Many times, he'll just have to learn to wait it out and consider the long-haul relationship with his children, as opposed to the short-term resentments he might feel about his former wife's tactics.*

*One fellow told me: "Through the years, I've learned patience. If I treat my kids right, they'll know. My home is always open to them."*

*And often, in later years, the children will seek out the father and want to live with him, particularly if the mother has spent years telling the kids what a louse he is.*

How much effect does all this infighting have on the children themselves? Often their age and sex will determine that. Dr. Don Lunde told us: "For children three and under, there's not that much need to worry; they really don't know what's going on. With kids in the 5 to 10 year age group, this preprogramming can be much more injurious, particularly if an only child is involved and if that only child is a girl. If the mother keeps talking about her former husband as a bastard, the girl will tend to accept what is being said and to identify with the mother. Then, in her early teens, there is often a reversal, a period of romanticizing, a breaking away. At this point, the child may run away from home and try to live permanently with her father."

The teen-agers present a completely different picture. If the parents live close by, they tend to run back and forth between households, pitting one set of parents against the other. Perhaps, they're trying to "get back" at both natural parents.

Dr. Ernest Pecci sums it up this way: "The teeners are only interested in their own peer group because they harbor resentments over the divorce. Their philosophy often is: 'Screw everybody but me.' They're apt to say to the stepfather: 'My real Dad is getting me a motorcycle for my birthday. What are you getting me?' They put all parents into a real guilt trap, in which they, the kids, are really making out like bandits."

While we're on the subject of "Games People Play"—and remember, they learned them all from us—*jealousy* often rears its head within a new stepfamily.

With regard to the new father and an adolescent step-daughter, for example, very often the remarried mother misinterprets her daughter's emotional ups and downs, which are the natural result of changes in the girl's body and her questions about her own sexuality, as being resentment of the man her mother married. And so the stepfather, the man in the house, becomes a sore point. But it has nothing to do with his step-marriage. It's just a normal adolescent problem.

Often a child and a parent fight for the love of the other spouse.

Actress Polly Bergen talked to us about the early days of her marriage to Freddie Fields when his daughter, Kathy, was living with them: "I think the only area of disagreement Kathy and I ever had was her high competitiveness with me for her father. So one day I just sat down on the steps with her and said: 'Look, it's perfectly normal for you to be very jealous of me. However, I can tell you, you just don't have a *chance* of winning. And, particularly the way you're doing it, which is to remain a child forever. You're growing up and you're going to have to start thinking of yourself as an adult.'

"That was really the only strong confrontation Kathy and I ever had. And I've always treated her as if she were my own. In fact, after Freddie and I had children of our own, *all* the children, past and present, seemed to relate beautifully to one another."

How do kids themselves get along with each other: his versus hers? Usually pretty good. One of the best arrangements is when an "only" child visits a multiple-child household. This is the situation we find ourselves in when Ellen visits us. The only child often longs to be part of a larger household, to be one of an "organized mob." Dr. Lunde points out this is a most attractive situation: a dream fulfillment complex.

Ellen loves her second home, yet knows that after a while, she'll go back to her mother where she can also enjoy the advantages that "one and only" receives.

The more stepparents we talked to, the more we realized that his versus hers is, indeed, a minor problem. Children can make it with children. In fact, without the hang-ups that adulthood brings, this entire chapter on resentments would probably not even be necessary.

But let's get back to our super sage figures, the grown-ups, and most particularly, to good old Dad and some of the problems *he* can cause.

It's Sunday and time to visit Daddy. Sure, many ex-wives will force a child to sit on the front doorstep waiting for his father to pick him up so that no social contact is necessary. But still, does that give any man the right to keep his child waiting for hours? We heard of one situation where a child sat in front of his locked front door for *six hours!* How about that for cruel and inhumane treatment? Maybe it was the father's way of rebelling agaisnt the divorce, the alimony, the child support, the whole hassle; but it was the *child* who suffered. And yet we expect these same kids to grow up feeling good about themselves and respecting their elders.

A Dad has another method of rebelling that's possibly more cruel. In *Inside Divorce* authors Edmond Addeo and Robert Berger point out that in Los Angeles County, *it is estimated that 90 percent of the fathers do not take advantage of any of the visitation rights they received in their dissolutions and which they hold out to their children as a promise.* There is *no* contact. None. To these men, their children no longer exist.

What about the man who remarries and becomes a stepfather to someone else's children?

We have heard of situations where the stepfather violently resents his stepchildren because they look like "him," the natural father, and because the kids are a constant reminder that some other man's sperm created them, that some other man had "made it" with his wife.

Meanwhile, the natural father continues lashing out at everybody while wondering where all his child support checks are going. He may want his son to take part in Little League, or Pop Warner football; and he may personally insist on supervising the whole shmeer. This involves his being in and out of the household much more than the current husband wants. And the child himself may not care about sports any longer, having now been exposed to the interests and expertise of his new male parental figure, so he's quite confused.

Even with periodic visits, the ex-husband may feel he is

losing control, and that his children are only going through the motions of enjoyment when they are with him. A child may slip and refer to his stepdad as "Daddy," a blow to the natural father's pride.

One 11-year-old girl we talked to spoke of her summer vacations with her Dad as "OK." She said: "It's glamorous enough. We go on trips all over the country, and once we went to Europe. But still, there is no *family* there. I can't wait to get home."

As years go by, the biological father may want to guide his childrens' schooling and attend the parent-child functions. If the stepfather feels this responsibility too, something's got to give. Otherwise, the child is put into the impossible situation of trying to please everybody but himself.

And so the male ego trip goes on. We know of one father who drops by the new household once in a while to "look at his furniture." His main resentment is money, and he can't stand to see the new guy lounging on *his* sofa.

In fact, for many people, money leads to more resentments than all of the jealous infighting combined.

The divorce itself probably was the single biggest financial strain that the previous marriage ever experienced. *Money* magazine, in trying to figure out the costs of divorce, advises the former husband to be prepared to live on about half his former income after divorce. Resentments? You betcha! Now he has the additional costs of maintaining two households, paying double taxes, child support, and all the legal fees he's just been through. To many men, the welfare of the children seems to take second place to their rapidly depleting pocketbooks.

Now, what about the new husband, the new stepfather? Can he plan on the natural father's child support payments to help him maintain the current household? In most cases, not by the hair of your chinny chin chin.

*Only about 15 percent of child support payments, nation-wide, are kept current. In other words, 85 percent of the*

*natural fathers either skip out of or are terribly delinquent in*
*their child support payments.*

In *Inside Divorce*, the authors point out just how bad this
situation has gotten. One new stepfather, in financial straits,
applied for a bank loan, listing his wife's child support
payments as regular income. The banker laughed at him; the
loan was refused.

Clearly, financial institutions have taken the realistic view
that alimony and child support are more precarious than a
first-time job. Back breaking payments to an ex-family are the
easiest obligations to rationalize away. For the word "money,"
substitute "survival."

What about the current and ex-wives, the recipients of all
this loot? Again, resentments abound, depending on whose
side you're on.

**Owen:** *One recent radio show brought these three calls in a*
*row, with three completely different points of view.*

**Caller 1:** Owen, this is Lee. My husband and I have been
supporting his three children for years. Now,
there's a new law that says a child is an adult
at 18, but his divorce occurred *before* that law.
So, unless the state of California changes something, we're stuck paying for those kids until
they're 21. We're in quite a hassle now with his
ex-wife. Look, either you're an adult at 18 or
you're not. This is ridiculous. I mean, we both
work and just when we looked forward to some
easier years, now we're saddled with another
three years of support that will break our
backs. We'd like to help the kids all we can,
but not at the current rate of $600 a month.
And the ex-wife won't compromise one iota.

**Caller 2:**   I just heard her. Why should we compromise? I have a son almost 18 now. He can't get a job, with the recession and all. And do you know what the cost of living has done to us receiving child support? It's killing us. Screw the poor second wife.

**Caller 3:**   Owen, look, I've been through one divorce, two annulments, and a dissolution. I have four kids from one of these partnerships or another. And, if I've never accomplished one other thing, I've drummed independence into each of my kids. I've had them all working at one job or another since they were 14. I explained that ours was not the usual permanent family relationship, and that looking out for yourself was one of the greatest things they could learn. They're all self-sufficient now and earning their own incomes. Why should I demand money from a man I hardly even know anymore?

Three totally diverse points of view about money, one of the roots of all resentments. Maybe you saw yourself in number one, number two, number three, or none of the above.

One couple we talked to admitted to some rough sledding in their early years of marriage not only because of money, but because of differing views of what the money was for.

Let's call them Ann and Bob. He inherited three of her children while supporting two more of his own. After they were married, Ann kept working as a secretary, while complaining that she was just a middleman for her salary check which went to cover his child support obligations. And she never let Bob forget it.

Today, Ann realizes that she should have entered that marriage fully aware of Bob's previous financial obligations and that her salary plus Bob's income should have been considered as *total* assets versus *total* family liabilities. Even though the dollar outcome at each month's end was the same, a change of viewpoint toward money could have brought a more peaceful early relationship.

Even geography can play a part in determining the success of a stepmarriage.

Custody officials say that the closer the ex and current families live, the more problems one might expect. Proximity seems to fan the flame of anger.

One stepfather put it this way: "My wife would love to see her 'ex' move the hell out of town, and so would I. We'd like to eliminate him from our lives. We do very well as a family. The children are affectionate and devoted to me, and we're interested in doing things together. The only time we ever argue is when the natural father interferes with our way of doing things."

Have we been luckier than most and avoided most of these pitfalls of resentment in our marriage? Hardly. One way or another, we've probably had to handle more than our share. But we have tried to be very open about discussing our former marriages with our children, pointing out that none of us is perfect.

If we've learned one thing about stepparenthood, it's *never* criticize a child's natural parent in front of that child.

We've learned a much more constructive device from Dr. Ernest Pecci, who advises talking to a stepchild this way: "Look, your Mother loves you very much and I love you, too. You can love both of us and it's okay. When you're with your Mother, you love her, and you don't have to say good things about me if you don't want to. Be true to yourself."

In this kind of dialogue, you eliminate the competitive aspect and elevate feelings to a more mature level. Kids care about themselves: "What's going to happen to *me*?" They're not interested in adult games, but they'll sure learn them from us, unless we, as parents, talk out these problems as they happen.

Writer Edmond Addeo told us about a new type of encounter weekend, strictly for happily married couples.

What is it? It's not awareness and group-groping and all that. It's a retreat for married couples. You go on a Friday night, without children or telephones. You don't talk to any other couples. It's just you and your wife. No psychologists in attendance. And it's 44 hours with no alcohol. It's an intense training in a new communications technique. And it's only for *happily* married couples. It's not to save a marriage. It's not to give you new insights into swinging new fads. If you have a bad marriage, this type of encounter is *not* for you.

Explained Mr. Addeo, "You are with about 25 other couples. You all get a presentation from several other couples who've been through this before, and who want to share their experiences with you. Then, either the wife or the husband goes to the room. The other stays in kind of a study hall. And you write love letters to each other. After that's over, you read each other's letters alone. And then, together, you go over the message that each of you has just written to the other, and you discuss it. You talk about it. It doesn't sound like that big a deal, but it's an overwhelming experience. It really is. It opens up a whole new world of communication with your wife, or your husband.

We just went to one, my wife and I. We've been married for 15 years, in what I consider one of the great all-time marriages. And my marriage now is infinitely better than it was. You can get information from the local churches. But it is not run *by* the clergy. It's run by the couples themselves."

Carol, a 30-year-old housewife fairly new to the step-marriage scene, writes letters too, but with a different idea in mind: "Sure there are things my new husband does that bug the hell out of me. But when I'm really angry, I sit down at a typewriter and let it all hang out. I really lash out and say all the horrible things I feel. Then, I take the letter over to the fireplace and burn it. It's out of my system."

Robert Berger added another touch to this system: "Our roughest marital days were in the beginning, the first few years. Since I was a young writer, I always had a typewriter around. What we used to do when we really got mad would be to go to the typewriter, state our arguments and anything else we had on our minds. Then, leave. The other one would come over, read what was written on the typed page, sit down, and reply. We'd argue, on the typewriter, and it was tremendously therapeutic."

So, we're back to the single most important preventative to resentments — communication, either spoken or written. And it works, or at least it should, unless you could envision the following situation.

One spouse sits down at the typewriter and comes up with something like this: "I think you're the most egotistical, selfish, son-of-a-bitch I've ever seen. You're arrogant. You care nothing about my children, and I hate you."

An hour later, one single line appears on the typewriter in response: "The same to you."

# Resentments Revisited over a Club Sandwich

**Owen:**  *We settled into a booth amid the noises of the typical businessman's noontime restaurant.*

*Drinks were ordered, and we admired the view.*

*Both were exceedingly good. We relaxed.*

*Then we got down to money.*

*If one could sum up all the resentments in the stepfamily relationship in their order of importance, money would probably rank in the number one spot.*

*Ongoing financial obligations from previous marriages, both to the giver and the receiver, help keep those old bitter juices flowing: the ex-husband who wonders what the hell is happening to all of his support payments, and the ex-wife who feels it isn't enough or why doesn't the check arrive on time?*

*I think it was money that finally brought Dean Anderson and me together in this long-overdue talk session. Father and stepfather. Face to face. Las Vegas's Jimmy the Greek listed the odds as 5-4, and you pick 'em.*

*Actually, Dean and I had known each other for years during our former marriages so our meeting wasn't like that of two strangers. But regardless of a prior acquaintance I recommend a meeting like this. It clears the air.*

**Nancie:** *Don't leave the women out. Mothers should meet eye to eye, too. It could dispel the fantasies we have about each other, and force us to participate on a more realistic level.*

**Owen:** *Through the years Dean had expressed a very natural concern for how his checks were being spent. Were they only for his childrens' welfare or was our stepfamily living it up on his dough?*

*What man wouldn't wonder when he sees his ex-wife and her husband fly off to an exotic spot like the Middle East while finding his daughter in threadbare jeans?*

*So, finances occupied the drinks and appetizer portion of our infamous lunch.*

*Dean explained his financial position as a man in business for himself, and how difficult it is for him to send that monthly check on time when he is waiting for others to pay him. And he asked what his kids were getting out of it all.*

*I explained my side of it: I have inherited a whole raft of financial obligations with his children, regardless of the child support. Example: Nancie and I are living in a much larger house than the two of us would ever have needed, with corresponding expenses and taxes precipitated by "the good school district."*

*I pointed out my other out-of-pocket expenses: taking his kids out to dinner, and buying groceries on my own. (How else can I sneak in all those "junk food" specials under the watchful eyes of Nancie Nutrition?)*

**Nancie:** *This is not inconsistent with what I said in Chapter 5 about **my** paying for **my** children when we go out to dinner. Some weeks my budget won't take the expense so Owen gallantly comes through or we stay home.*

**Owen:** *I mentioned the domino tournaments Peter and I enter at $50 a throw, Ashley's weekly allowance, plus the much too frequent visits by the tooth fairy.*

*We laughed over that, but we both pretty much laid bare our financial positions, including my child support and transportation obligations to Ellen. I further explained to Dean that these occasional flamboyant trips we took were really working press excursions and cost us very little, one of the few advantages of being in the business I'm in.*

*Dean expressed the most concern about his teenager, Chris, who was approaching 16. Even without the steprelationship this can be a trying period.*

*Dean felt I was not exercising enough discipline with Chris, and I agreed. I was much more secure in my authoritarian role with the two younger ones than I was with Chris. With him, or with any young adult, as a stepfather I was simply not sure of how far I could go.*

*"Look, I'll do my best. I'll sit down and have a long talk with Chris. It's about time anyway since he's now into cars, girls, and parties. Let me give it a try."*

*We ended a two-hour lunch that should have taken place earlier, but didn't.*

*Dean remarked, "Any criticism I've had is not nearly as important as the fact that you've made Nancie happy and created a good home for my children. I want you to know I appreciate that. And I'll always support you in any decision you make regarding the day-to-day lives of my children."*

*I'm not saying that we have solved all the problems that the future may bring, but we've made one giant step. If future problems do arise, I think Dean and I can arrive at a solution much more quickly.*

*Father and stepfather, acting like adults, communicating and coping.*

*By the way, Chris and I had that long talk.*
*"What would you change in this family to make it better?"*
*Chris replied, "Discipline. We don't have rules that apply to everybody."*

*"You're right. But once we start with more discipline, fair to all, you're the one who's going to get it more than anyone else. In some areas, you're the one who's been getting away with murder, because I really didn't know how much authority you'd take from me."*

*"Just so it's fair to all of us. That's what's important,"* replied our teen-ager.

*"Okay, how else can we improve things?"*

*Chris went on to express his dismay that we don't do things as a family—an all-day outing, a project. "How about hiking in the country, all of us?"*

*At the dinner table that night, I broached the idea of togetherness to all concerned.*

| | |
|---|---|
| **Peter:** | I hate hiking. |
| **Ashley:** | I'd rather go to a movie. |
| **Peter:** | How about going to a baseball game? |
| **Chris:** | Baseball bores me. |
| **Ashley:** | I'd rather go to a movie. |

*We spent 37 minutes and 9 seconds trying to find one area that interested everybody. When it got down to 3 to 2 on skydiving, we closed the discussion and cleared the dishes. We did agree, though, that the following Saturday we would, at least, try hiking and that no one should make any other plans for that date.*

*Saturday arrived.*

*Dean called and invited the boys over for the weekend.*

*After we dropped them off, we took Ashley to an "R" rated movie.*

*In the rain.*

*Maybe next Saturday.*

# Legal Leftovers: His

Once your divorce was over, you figured you were finished with lawyers and courts and battling, right?

Wrong.

What about the other children, the children who will not be living in the household? In most cases, it's the Father's kids involved here.

Probably they are still living with their Mother, who may not be terribly overjoyed that her former husband has found happiness in a new marriage. She may very well find ingenious ways in which to pass on her resentments (both subliminal and overt) to those children. We'll go into these various forms of one-upmanship later.

Right now, however, we're discussing the law.

New York psychiatrist, Dr. Lee Salk, talks about how the law can be used to prevent a child from enjoying the companionship of both parents.

He says: "Because of the way divorce laws are practiced in this country, children are put right in the middle, where they are often used as hostages, for a parent to get more money, or as a vehicle for their own desires and schemes."

Other experts pick up the ball here and go even further. They feel that, to prevent a child from being put in this position, the custodial parent should have full "say so" as to raising that child, that the custodial parent should have full control as to whether or not the child ever sees the other parent.

We simply cannot buy this theory. Under such a system, you are taking away the child's identity completely, and, in effect, depriving one parent of his rights. The man is relegated to the status of being an absent check sender.

But most divorce settlements do allow the father "reasonable visitation rights."

This one phrase, "reasonable visitation rights," can mean very different things to different people.

**Owen:**   *What is reasonable? To the Father, it would logically mean sharing Christmas, Easter, and summer vacations, and, if the families live close-by, alternating weekends.*

*But to the natural mother, seething over her former mate's newly found happiness (and built-in family), it can mean: half-a-day on alternate Tuesdays, every other month, if the moon is full.*

*Attorney Arden Weinberg asks: "How are people who were not able to live with one another as man and wife, going to be 'reasonable' in one of the most sensitive areas?*

*"I urge my clients to establish some ground rules right at the beginning. I ask them 'What's the minimum kind of thing you both can be comfortable with here at the beginning? We can always change it later, but let's get specific right at the start.'"*

*If what is reasonable can't be worked out between two so-called reasonable people, then you have only one recourse: back to your attorney and back to the courts.*

*You are, in effect, asking the court to spell out, exactly, what is sensible, something you should have insisted on when the original divorce agreement was being worked out. But you didn't, did you, dummy? You were so anxious to get the whole thing over with, you agreed to sign anything.*

*Now, it's going to cost you some money. Accept it. Not only that, but don't be surprised if your former wife, in retaliation, counter sues you for more child support. This is a rather common ploy, used in the hope that you'll call off your end of the battle.*

*I think you might need a note of optimism at this point, now that your palms are sweating a little.*

*You've gone this far. Don't back down. Child support payments are, pretty much, based on mathematical formula, so unless you've suddenly found yourself in a much higher economic bracket, the odds are really on your side.*

*Chances are, you'll win. She'll lose. The judge will grant specific periods of the year for visitation and will turn down her request for more dough.*

*Sure, it's a hassle. But, in the event the two families no longer live anywhere near each other, it's something that has to be done. Otherwise, you'll find yourself sending off monthly checks to support an anonymous child that you'll never see again, or hear from. And that can be a drain, both financially and emotionally.*

**Nancie:** *I see this from a totally different vantage point, that of an observer in a courtroom. When Owen had to go before a judge to obtain the right to see his daughter on a regular basis, I audienced the drama. I was never asked by his attorney to participate, although I think I was objective enough to be able to see what was going to cause problems later.*

*We asked the court for permission to have Ellen live with us for a month in summer, the Easter holiday, and every other Christmas vacation. Ellen's mother said "No" to Christmas, so the judge compromised, which is apparently about all our domestic legal system feels comfortable doing, whether it's to the betterment or detriment of the people involved. He ruled that we were to share the two weeks, with Ellen always spending Christmas Eve and Christmas Day with her mother.*

*I feel the decision is to the detriment of all of us. And I thought so that day in court.*

*It's a thorn that never stops jabbing.*

*When Ellen lived in New York, her mother used to write us in October that, because the weather in New York would be bad on December 27, and the roads to the airport would be closed, and San Francisco would be fogged in (and Ellen's plane would be diverted to 'God knows where'), it would be so much better for Ellen to stay in New York with the airfare being spent, instead, on gifts for her and a long phone call on Christmas Day. She also stated that the trip was very tiring for the child and it would be wise to be more considerate of her health. When we suggested alternating years for the whole vacation (as we asked originally), there was no more talk about Ellen's well-being.*

**Owen:** *There is another legal aspect to this matter of child visitation which I hate to even bring up, because it can involve one more court appearance, which is all you need right now, right?*

*If (God forbid!) the natural mother is a truly vindictive person, she can petition the court that these newly won visits are causing the child "emotional strain," that the child is becoming shattered at the thought of visiting that "other" household with that "other" woman and her children.*

*This is pure baloney and can be put at rest with one session with a psychologist, appointed by the court, and usually found in a county's custody department. After a brief interview with both father and child, the psychologist can easily conclude that nobody is being destroyed and that the child does look forward to visiting Dad and stepfamily. Letters to that effect then go out to all concerned, and that ends that.*

*A final note on child visitation. The court psychologist may
also warn: "Look, you've been through this whole legal mess.
You've won. Never, never give up what you've won. Through
the years (if the child lives far away), you'll be told he or she
has developed other friendships and interests . . . and
considers it an intrusion to be forced to spend time with you.
Don't ever buy this line, or, suddenly the original parent can
claim you don't care anymore. Your visits are legally spelled
out. Stick to them."*

*And the counselor is right. Sure, your own child, living in
another part of the country, may want to spend Christmas
with friends.*

*But once he or she gets off that plane, into your arms, and
into the lives of his other family, you'll see a grin a mile wide.*

**Nancie:**   *There comes a time in a remarriage when the
hassling with the ex-wife about the children can get to be too
much for the father. When he reaches this low ebb, he can
quite easily be manipulated by his new spouse into letting go a
little ("Why fight it?") and can be urged to relinquish more
and more involvement in the lives of his absent children. The
new stepmother can maneuver him into activities with her
children and/or with their own offspring that overshadow his
feeling of responsibility for the others.*

*I have seen this game played so subtly that the poor father
lost his kids altogether before he ever knew what happened.
And the stepmother no longer had to be one.*

*Of course, today she is no longer his wife, either.*

Let's consider one other situation where you thought the
divorce was final, but the maladies linger on.

The wife remarries. The former husband, paying through
the nose for child support, demands an accounting of how his
money is being spent. Is it going for food, clothing, and shelter
for his kids, or for steak and beer for the new husband?

Now the law works in a different way.

Can he get this financial accounting? The answer is simple. No.

An attorney explained it to us this way: "Look. How can you apportion the childrens' share of a household? We're not just talking about food, but also their share of the living room, water and gas bills, and the telephone. It's impossible. Forget it."

Not only can't a father ask for a legal accounting of his child support money, most times he can't even expect a written or verbal accounting of his child's progress.

**Nancie:** *I really do feel mothers who receive support checks should accept the responsibility of reporting to the father on a child's development in school, his growth at home, and his financial requirements.*

*Actually, this is not a holier-than-thou declaration as I've been caught in this trap myself. On one particular occasion the father of my children was asking me where all his money went. I gave a rather hysterical report on the previous months' mounting bills, not letting him forget what a conscientious and talented handler of money I was. He let me run down and then, very calmly, he spoke: "My, you sound good enough to marry." Not only did he burst my balloon with good humor, it also kept us both in line for a while after that.*

One legal counselor pointed out that there is another type of natural father who looks on this monthly check as the end of his responsibilities. He is relieved to send off the money and not have to deal with the raising of the kids. He wants off the hook. When school problems arise and Mom wants to involve him, it's a way to duck out and say: "Well, you have a husband now. Let him take care of it."

Some men can assume financial responsibilities better than emotional responsibilities.

Another problem area that might arise is where the natural father disapproves of the new life-style of his former wife and her mate.

Suppose his kids are now being raised in a hippie household, or his wife has taken up a Far Eastern religion, and the whole family has shaved their heads and begun singing on street corners?

What can the father do? Nothing, as far as that household is concerned. His only recourse is to go for complete custody of the children.

And, if he's a millionaire and can hire a top divorce attorney, he does stand a chance of getting his children out of that new household.

Otherwise, he has no real legal say-so at all.

To show what ridiculous lengths some of these legal battles have reached, a lawyer friend told us this story about one of his recent court cases.

He said: "I'm representing a father who is divorced from his wife. She has the kids. She has turned into a tournament bridge freak and spends all her time going from one bridge game to another. The result: she is at home with the kids very little. She also has a new male "friend," a bridge hustler who moves in and out of the house at will. Finally, my client, the father, said to the wife: 'The next time you go away, let me baby sit my own kids. Give me first refusal. I'll do it for free.'

"She replied in so many words: 'Screw you, fella.'

"They ended up in the judge's chambers—the wife, the father, the hustler, and the two attorneys. The subject, supposedly, was the life-style of the woman. But the argument finally got around to whether or not her lover would be allowed 'shack up' privileges one night a week.

"By now the judge realized the total absurdity of the entire situation and threw them all out of court. But my client didn't get the satisfaction of either getting his kids back or effecting any promise on her part for a change in life-styles."

No, unfortunately, that divorce decree is often not as final as you'd like it to be.

But it helps to know your rights. It also helps to know when you don't have a chance at all.

There is one other most important legal leftover that should be attended to immediately! Your will!

Your new family life is settling down into a harmonious routine. Everyone is adjusting to the new relationships. And, obviously, no one wants to even consider the possibility of death.

But just remember this. If not replaced, that old will of yours could be like a time bomb!

Just let this one statement sink in for a moment: *It has been held by case law that divorce does* not *revoke a will.* (In re Brannon's estate, Ill Cal. App. 38, 295 Pac. 83.)

That means that whatever estate planning (wills, insurance policies, etc.) you had previously arranged is still in effect.

Should you die tomorrow, your previous spouse, on behalf of her children, is most likely to inherit a great portion of what you have worked so hard to build up.

Divorce does not revoke a will. Remarriage does. But that still doesn't prevent your previous spouse from contesting the estate on behalf of her, or his, children.

By all means, the newly married couple should see an attorney together and discuss all aspects of past and future finances. With the likelihood of two sets of children involved, plan on a rather long session. It can save a lot of heartache later.

Reexamine all existing insurance, not just the life insurance policies, but everything: pension and welfare plans, auto club death benefits, etc. Make sure these monies go where you want them to go.

Lay it all out — who owns what, as of the beginning of the marriage, and who gets what in the event of death. List all the children specifically and what you would like each of them to receive.

If there is one child not to be included in a share of the estate, say so in the will: "That as of such and such a date, you feel that your possible Black Sheep should receive the total sum of one dollar." This can be changed at any later date if the situation should improve.

The most common type of will in a stepmarriage is for one spouse to leave all to the remaining spouse, with specific instructions on how his or her children should be taken care of. Thus, the remaining spouse acts as the executor of the estate.

Most important, plan for all contingencies in the event of a mutual disaster, if both you and your spouse should be killed together. Without proper outlines, this could result in the biggest court mish-mash of all times, with ex-spouses all claiming their shares of the estate on behalf of their original children.

Make sure an outside executor is named to administer the estate in the event of a mutual disaster. Most attorneys recommend a bank for this function.

Do *not* appoint an older child in this capacity, even if he has achieved his majority. In addition to dividing up the monies involved, the children will also be dividing up the household furnishings and personal possessions. And this is where most family battles take place. Imagine two daughters (step and natural) quibbling over lamps, sofas, paintings, etc., while an older brother tries to referee a stepfamily infight. It just isn't worth it.

The time to plan for your future is today, the moment you enter into your new marriage, particularly, if various sets of children are involved.

You worked and saved a long time to get what you have today. Make sure it goes where you want it to go.

# Solution: A Loving Divorce

"Our relationship has never been in question. It's always been the outside interferences, the garbage left over from our first marriages."

This was the reply we got from a very rational, middle-aged stepfather when we asked him what the problems were in his recent marriage. And this is what we've heard from others, too: how the resentments, parental downgrading, hurts and guilts from the past carried over into their current mergers.

It then appears that we must return to the divorce process itself to realize that this is where everything starts. This is the origin of future difficulties.

We have reached a point in the United States where we must seriously consider reform in two major fields: (1) the legal arena, which makes adversaries of us all, and (2) the emotional arena, which creates the inner hostilities that can turn us into our own worst enemies. In fact, let's take a look at this second battle first.

A divorce without bitterness is a rare bird.

**Owen:** *The following conversation took place on my radio show in late April of 1975, between Dr. Ernest Pecci, the psychiatrist we quoted earlier who is head of the Center for Psycho-Spiritual Integration, the radio listeners, and myself.*

*The subject: How to have a loving divorce.*

**Caller:**  Dr. Pecci, I think you're out of your mind, talking about a loving divorce. My husband and I are going through a divorce now, and it's turned into a three-ring circus. Everybody has taken sides: in-laws, grandparents, the children. Each of us has an attorney who says we must not communicate with our ex-spouse. It's like two armies on a battlefield. It's a nightmare. It's unreal.

**Dr. Pecci:**  Now, wait a minute. Forget the two armies. If I can get just one of you, you or your husband, to regain your self-respect, to remain calm and recall the positive aspects of your marriage, it will rub off. It will decrease the steam tremendously.

**Caller:**  Doctor, you can't talk to *one* of us. You'd have to talk to two armies. My husband and I don't feel the hostility near as much as the two families do. But we're not even allowed to speak to one another. The lawyers say "absolutely no contact." We might even have a chance for a reconciliation without all this interference. But, as I said, it's a nightmare.

**Dr. Pecci:**  Who is it that's particularly hostile, your mother-in-law?

**Caller:**  Yes.

**Dr. Pecci:**  She may well be living out her own hostility, her own unresolved problems through you. But just as you must learn and be able to grow from this divorce experience, you must allow her that same chance to grow. Call your mother-in-law. Confront her. Ask her what *she* wants. Say to her: "I am taking full responsibility for this divorce. I know you're hurt from what you think I did to your son. But this is what I feel is best for me." Then say to her: "What do you want me to do? Do you want me to divorce him, not to divorce him? Do you want me to kill myself? What do you want?"

You'll find often she won't know what she wants. But let her unload. Let her transfer to you all her problems of the past. Let her get rid of the stuff she's been keeping in her gut for years. And let her dump it all on you. But you stay calm. Assure her: "I understand that you're hurting. But I'm doing what I feel is best for me." You'll be surprised how quickly her hostilities disappear.

**Owen:** Before we can get to the point of reprogramming ourselves emotionally for that loving divorce, we must understand what marriage is, originally.

**Dr. Pecci:** A marriage is a contract, a commitment. When you marry, you're asking for the love that, perhaps, you didn't get from your parents. You say to yourself: "It's going to work." However, often your mate is totally unaware of what's being demanded of him, through lack of communication.

When a couple comes into my office, I ask them to write down a list of what they had originally expected of one another. Often (and this is during the divorce stage) they will actually laugh when they read each other's list. The demands had been totally unreal, and neither could have possibly lived up to the other's expectations.

So here we have two emotionally insecure people trying to have their needs fulfilled, even though each may be totally unaware of what those needs are. We become disappointed and start blaming one another. We see all the negative attributes of our own parents coming out in our mate—all the horrible things we hated as kids. Then, we go on and magnify those faults. And we ask ourselves: "How could we ever have married that person?"

**Owen:** The emotion we had in the love relationship, in the exact level of intensity, turns into the hate relationship.

**Dr. Pecci:** And yet beyond all this resentment, is a strong bond of the years of marriage together. If we don't cut this bond, we haven't cut the resentments, which will then stay with us long after the actual divorce.

We want our kids, our relatives to line up on our side to prove we're OK. Somebody has to be wrong. We say to ourselves and our families: "Either I'm unlovable or he's unlovable. Be on my side."

A loving divorce recognizes that the marriage has become a bad experience, that it's led to destructive patterns in both partners, and that it's just not a good idea to continue it. It's better to split, but only when you both realize the bond has to be cut.

We must acknowledge our weaknesses, too, in the marriage, instead of covering up for them, and recognize that there was no way to deal with them within that marital structure.

We must see that, although we cannot continue to live with one another, there is no reason we cannot have respect for one another.

**Caller:** Doctor, what if one partner is ready for a loving divorce and is ready to let go, but the other isn't?

**Dr. Pecci:** Don't get caught up in the emotion of your ex-spouse. If he wants to rant and rave, let him; but don't imitate him. Anger begets anger. Remain calm. Advise him: "I understand you're hurting, but I want to help you become free. I want to let you grow again, just as I am doing." If one of you can remain cool and relaxed, the other will begin using your attitude as a model.

**Owen:** Dr. Pecci also pointed out that, usually, bitterness increases after a divorce. We've been hurt. We build up a good case for ourselves on how much we hurt. And it's so easy to project this hostility on our kids and on our ex-spouse.

And, with all this hate, it is almost impossible for us to function as a good parent to our children. Furthermore, it's completely impossible for us to function as a good mate for someone else in a future marital situation.

**Dr. Pecci:** The emotional level at which you're operating prevents you from acting at a mature level within the new relationship. Your self-image is at rock bottom. Learn about yourself. Divorce is not the worst thing that can ever happen. Grow from the experience, and you'll find yourself in a very, very beautiful place.

**Owen:** *Sure enough, suddenly, the whole tenor of the phone calls started to change.*

**Caller:** My ex-wife and I get along really great, Doctor. We were married seven years. I'm 32; she's 29. We have two kids. But we finally realized that we were only staying together for the children's sakes. We resolved our differences and went our own ways. I've not remarried, but I am living with a great gal now.

**Owen:** And you don't get static from your ex-wife when the kids visit you and your new friend on weekends?

**Caller:** She doesn't say a word against me or my girl to our kids. Sure, after a weekend visit, she may question the children as to what my girl is like, but it's more like natural curiousity than prying.

**Owen:** So it's worked out well?

**Caller:** So well, that my ex-wife, who is a nurse, has even kept me on her medical plan. It's really a good relationship.

**Owen:** *And finally came this call from a middle-aged woman. It sounded like it came right out of Noel Coward's* Private Lives, *it was so sophisticated.*

**Caller:** I'd like to share with your listeners a very loving divorce of 23 years. Not only do I have a beautiful relationship with my former husband, but also with his wife. I consider the two of them to be my very dearest friends.

Not that it didn't take a great deal of maturity. My ex-husband married several years after we divorced, and his new wife knew that I was most anxious that this marriage take place. I was all on her side, perhaps, a bit selfishly. I thought that, if anything happened to me, there was a gal who would take care of my daughter.

**Dr. Pecci:** When did your marital problems start?

**Caller:** Oh, we'd been married about 20 years, and we both knew it wasn't working. I thought, because of our deep and profound feelings for one another, why not try to salvage something out of all this for each of our lives?

After the divorce, my child never heard one bad word about me from her dad, and only the best things about her father from me.

The only postmarital fight occurred years later, when we were drawn back together to plan our daughter's wedding. We fought over arrangements for the wedding and reception.

On the night before her wedding, my daughter said to me: "Mom, I just realized. You and Dad are like two parallel lines that could never meet. But that has never prevented me from loving you both."

Our daughter was finally able to look back and evaluate the whole lifetime situation, and her own marriage will be better for it.

**Owen:** Did you have any help along the way in this loving divorce?

**Caller:** The help I had, I needed like a hole-in-the-head. We made it despite attorneys and psychiatrists, who were suspicious at how easily we were handling things. They couldn't believe we had worked things out, and they felt something had to be wrong.

But we did make it, in spite of them. My husband's new wife? I call her my sister-in-law. My ex-husband is a very dear friend. We visit each other all the time.

We had a loving divorce. We still do. It can be done, but it takes a lot of work and a lot of conviction."

**Owen:** What better proof that it can be done, indeed? Again, if you say to yourself: "What's best for *me*? How can *I* grow again? What will make *me* happy?" And then, if you realize that the divorce paper is not enough, that you've got to cut, not only the legal bond, but the emotional bond, then you're well on your way.

You'll be so much better prepared to enter that stepmarriage situation, because you've been an honest, open human being. It will rub off on all around you, too—your new mate and your new brood of children.

And your mistakes of the past will be in the past, unlike those of this one last caller.

**Caller:** Owen, I guess I've had a lot of loving divorces.

**Owen:** What do you mean?

**Caller:** My husband and I have been divorced three time, and we've remarried every time.

**Owen:** You mean you've married the same man four times? When did it all start?

**Caller:** Well, we were married first when we were in our early twenties. Then, we'd get a divorce, separate for a year or so, and then get married again.

**Owen:** How old are you now?

**Caller:** I'm 48. My husband is 52.

**Owen:** How's it working out this time?

**Caller:** Just great. Although we do have separate bed-rooms.

**Owen:** That sounds like you're just two people living under the same roof.

**Caller:** Oh, no, we have sex.

**Owen:** Can I ask how often?

**Caller:** Twice.

**Owen:** Twice what?

**Caller:** Twice a year.

**Owen:** I've heard of loving divorces, but this is really ridiculous!

**Nancie:** *Years ago, even before my first marriage, while I was living in Los Angeles, I was invited to a Divorce Party. My dentist and his wife were splitting up. They wanted to gather together the friends of that marriage to announce: "Hey, although we're divorcing, it's OK. We still care enough about each of you to remain friends separately." I refused to go to that party. I thought the whole idea was sick. How wrong I was. They were just ahead of their time.*

# Solution: Let's Get Divorce Out of the Courts

**Owen:**   *One of the top divorce attorneys in Los Angeles told me quite bluntly over lunch: "If you give me a free hand, and if you're willing to spend the bucks, I'll get custody of your kid. I mean that. If you have unlimited money and don't mind being absolutely ruthless, I'll get your kid. And I won't be doing anything illegal; it will all be within the framework of the law."*

*I asked him: "What if the ex-spouse is leading an exemplary life, where you can't get her on anything?"*

*The answer: "I'll get her. You give me enough bucks, plenty of time, and a free hand, and I'll get custody for you."*

*The above statement, unfortunately, reflects on our court system at all levels. Certainly after Watergate most of us have come to the realization that money can indeed buy "justice," at least one kind of justice.*

*But it is this same thinking, this same battery of attorneys, and this same judicial system that gives birth to bitterness, fosters it, and lets it grow—long after a divorce is over.*

*In the last chapter, one caller complained of the two armies that had arisen, each with its own titular head from a law firm, that prohibited husband and wife from even simple communicating.*

*The woman who had affected a loving divorce had done so, if you remember, in spite of attorneys and psychiatrists.*

*Unfortunately, the law has created an adversary system out of what, basically, is a domestic problem. Changing the name from "divorce" to "dissolution" has not changed this adversary procedure one iota.*

*Changing the method of divorce from one party's admitting guilt (mental cruelty, adultery, etc.) to the new form of "no fault" litigation, again, has in no way altered the bitterness.*

*In fact, one lawyer told me: "Under no fault, there is more quarreling than ever. Since everything has to be split down the middle, couples are now fighting over lampshades and stereo tapes."*

*San Francisco divorce attorney Walter Winter feels there is an answer, even though it might take away his (and other divorce attorneys) livelihoods.*

*Mr. Winter says: "Divorce is the same as a business disagreement, much like that of a service station operator who wants to break his lease with his oil company. Two business partners disagree, right?*

*"Then let's not throw this situation into the same courts that handle murder, grand theft, personal injury, and robbery. It is impossible for divorce to be handled intelligently within a framework that only acknowledges adversary proceedings.*

*And, in fact, divorce courts are looked upon as the garbage cans of society."*

*Dr. Donald Lunde agrees and feels that neither the lawyers nor the judges, themselves, have any respect for these courts.*

*Dr. Lunde expressed it this way: "Most judges who sit in on domestic and juvenile courts are brand new in their jobs. Most often they are political appointees, who have had absolutely no training in human relations problems. They are very uncomfortable with their new situation and can't wait for seniority to get them out of domestic court, where they can really learn what it's like to 'play judge' at a higher judicial level. Most of these men look upon this first assignment as the waste-basket of the court system."*

*What are some of the other problems of today's legal system? For one, lack of uniformity from one county to another and from one judge to another.*

*One male friend of ours, recently divorced after a marriage of seven years, was ordered to pay $600 a month to his wife and two children.*

*Another friend, in front of a different judge, with no children and a marriage of just one year, had to come up with a $30,000 payoff to a woman he barely knew. Does that create bitterness? Does a chicken have feathers?*

*The failures of the courts today are numerous. Let's suppose the ex-spouse moves to another state and refuses to keep up the support payments. The former wife has a choice of four different court systems: her local superior or juvenile court, or the same two bodies in the husband's new state. Of course, she needs money to go to any of them. And she could end up with four different court decisions.*

*Get divorce out of our courts, and you'll get bitterness out of divorce.*

*Attorney Winter suggests that each state set up a department of family relations, manned by people knowledgable in the law, human psychology, domestic relations, and education. He explains: "This department would have a number of functions, only one of which would be judicial. It would involve counseling, before and after the divorce . . . and . . . education."*

*Let's talk about education for a moment. Where, in all of our schooling, are we ever trained to be marital partners or parents?*

*Walter Winter sees trained experts in these fields going to the schools to teach "Family Education." Says he, "Let's get rid of these P.E. teachers who've never been married, trying to teach kids about marriage."*

*Actually, in several Oregon schools, nine-week courses in marriage have recently been introduced. A young high school couple goes through the whole trip: a "mock wedding," shopping for a house, accruing the bills, arguing, getting into debt . . . right up until their "divorce" at the end of the course, which, by the way, is a loving divorce.*

*How would the department of family relations operate initially, when a couple first sought divorce?*

*The first step would be simple enough. The counselor would meet with the entire family, including the children. The couple would explain why they feel they would be happier living separately. If they had already reached an agreement on community property and the future of the children, the divorce would be granted.*

*If they couldn't agree on the problem of the children, there would be an independent investigation on the part of the department, much of which would involve talking with the children themselves.*

*But, here's the major point: Neither parent would be awarded custody of the child.*

*It might be decided that the child would live with the mother, for example, but the father would have equal access at any convenient time.*

*Let me repeat that. There would be no such thing as child custody. The child would live with one parent, but that parent would not have sole guiding authority over the child.*

*The department would continue to be involved in this situation after the divorce to oversee things.*

*No more would a mother be able to say: "Look, you no-good ex-husband, this kid is mine, and if you want to see him, you be here Sunday at exactly 10 A.M., and you have him back at exactly 6 P.M., period."*

*If both parents work they would each be asked to contribute to the support of the child.*

*Let's say, after the divorce, that the father still cannot get* satisfaction as to his visiting rights. Under the present adversary system, he must come up with the bucks necessary for a new hearing, which will then take him right back into the courtroom. Under the new procedure, for a small filing fee, he would go back to the department, walk up to a window, fill out a short form that says: "I want a hearing." This would set the wheels once again in motion. Everyone would then be called back in for a talk, and you wouldn't need a lawyer for any of this.

Under certain circumstances, during the divorce and investigation proceedings, the department might decide that neither parent should have physical custody, because of drug or alcohol problems, for instance, and that the child might be better off in a foster home, at least temporarily. But these cases would be the exception, not the rule.

In situations where the stepfather wants to adopt the children, again the department could fill his request, without forcing him to go through the expensive court process.

One of the most important aspects of this department of family relations would be in protecting the legal rights of the child. The department, remember, would offer an open door to all involved, long after that legal paper separates the two marital partners. If the mother remarries, and the child feels he is being ignored or mistreated by his new stepfather, he would have the right to come back and say: "Hey, I need a friend. I have a problem, and I want to talk about it."

Grandparents, cut off by the divorce and remarriage, could find an understanding listener within this new system, as well as the schools being given an opportunity to report back to the counselor when they see problems the divorce may have caused the child.

Just as educators now feel that a university should be open to people of all ages, so the department of family relations would maintain a lasting relationship with all the parties concerned.

*How would we pay for all of this? First, all monies currently being spent on our domestic court system and the judges therein would be reallocated to this family department. Second, all people using its services would be charged a reasonable fee, but certainly far under what is currently being spent on attorneys and court costs.*

*Sure, this does smack a little of big brotherhood, but our current procedure is so vastly imperfect, with financial and judicial inequalities, that it may be a small price to pay to end the bitterness that sometimes never ends in peoples' minds, and, therefore, in the minds of their offspring.*

*So much for child custody, you may ask, but how about money. How much would the poor ex-husband have to pay his ex-wife and their kids upon a divorce like this?*

*Ask yourself, what system do we have now? Earlier, we pointed out that one husband was asked to pay $600 a month for his wife and two children after a marriage of seven years, while the other, after a one year marriage and no children, had to come up with a settlement of $30,000.*

*Anything that eliminates this complete injustice will be a step in the right direction.*

**Walter:** Let's apply a uniformity, a schedule much like workmen's compensation. Taken into consideration would be the length of the marriage, the age of the couple, the age and number of children, the earning capacity of both parents. These mathematical tables would spell it out in black and white. There would be one absolute answer. There would be no quibbling, nor would you have to worry about one wacko judge.

**Owen:** But under this set-up, there would also be no need for the likes of you, the divorce attorneys?

**Walter:** Well, let's say, the schedule lists the wife as

eligible for support as a C-3. She just might want a lawyer to try to raise her category to a C-2.

**Owen:** Then we haven't accomplished anything.

**Walter:** Look, I'm kidding. Put this system in and we will be through. But I'm not really that worried, because this whole idea of change will not happen overnight. In fact, it's not going to happen in my working lifetime. As it stands now, I've made a lot of money on divorce, and I shall continue to make a lot of money on divorce.

There's one other thing that bugs the hell out of me with regard to our present court system, complete with the judge in the black robe. I would demand the immediate elimination of divorces from the "vital statistics" column in the daily newspapers. What happens in a marital separation between you and your wife is your private affair and has no business in the public notices of your morning paper.

**Owen:** *Why have we gone into such details in the past two chapters about the legal and emotional battlefields that most of us have gone through?*

*Because that's where it starts, festers, and grows: resentments, guilts, and fears that carry over into our present relationships with our new mates and our new stepchildren. And it's here the battle has to be won. We must be able to cut our previous bonds before we are ready to grow again, feel again, and love again.*

*One new stepfather told us: "My new marriage would be absolutely perfect, if it weren't for the garbage left over from the last one."*

# Adoption: The Ultimate Commitment

Generally, when one thinks of adoption one envisions taking on an orphaned child begotten and abandoned by strangers. The stepparent knows another side of the coin, however; and when the decision is made to share the legal, moral, and financial responsibilities of the spouse's offspring, the commitment is the ultimate positive in the stepfamily relationship.

Child custody officers love to see it happen.

Lawyers enjoy handling the paper work.

Each of them is exposed to so much of the splitting of families that the idea of putting a family together is a genuine reward of the trade.

Psychiatrists admit this is a time of tremendous pride and happiness for the child, as well.

What is an adoption?

A dictionary definition lists it as "the legal act whereby an adult person takes a minor into the relation of a child."

So much for dictionaries.

We feel the real rationale for adoption should be loving a child so much that he is a part of you. What came before can be erased as easily as his previous birth certificate. And the old joke, "*Your* child? I thought he was *my* child!" becomes the reality. Your eyes no longer see a difference.

105

Who adopts and why?

The question of adoption usually comes up in the first few years of remarriage if it is going to come up at all, because children do have a way of growing and leaving home. It's now or never.

A friend of ours, recently remarried, confided to us, "I'd adopt my wife's kids in a minute if we could get permission from her ex-husband." But in talking with him further we discovered the natural father is a bone of contention in the house. Our newly wed is having arguments with his wife over the children's visits with their father on weekends, and there is a mutual downgrading game being played.

It seems to us that it would be important for any stepfather contemplating adoption to ask himself honestly, "Do I want these children as my own because I really love them, or because it is the one legal way I have of eliminating their father from my household?"

Women, too, may tend to obscure the true issue. Several psychiatrists have told us of instances where the mother nags and nudges her new husband into adopting her children as a means of proving his complete devotion to her. He sometimes acquiesces for her peace of mind. Unfortunately, her peace of mind may lead to his going to pieces over the added financial burden or, in the event this second marriage disintegrates, supporting children he barely knows and rarely sees.

Attorney Arden Weinberg commented on these potential adoption problems: "At the point a couple comes into an attorney's office to seek an adoption, the lawyer doesn't know what type of reasoning preceded their decision. But we do our best to try to find out. Any of these feelings may well show up during the investigation by the probation or welfare agencies. In order for an adoption to go through there has to be a family evaluation done, followed by a recommendation by the agency. If it really is a questionable situation, the family will be advised to reevaluate what they want."

The agencies are not infallible, though, as we found out when a well-known attorney friend of ours told us this bizarre story.

Not too long ago he represented a stepfather who was asking to have an adoption annulled.

Here's how it came about.

The man had married a woman with two children. The natural father was sort of a drifter, but when he was in town, he would come around to see his sons.

He consented to an adoption, and the courts obliged.

Along with urging her second husband, a real estate investor, to adopt her children, the woman talked him into putting all his properties into both their names, supposedly for tax purposes.

Meanwhile, the natural father continued to see the children very secretly, and the children still considered him to be their parent although they kept that fact from their adoptive father.

A year later, the woman sued the real estate investor for divorce, collecting half the community property. He then went to court asking to have the adoption set aside on the grounds of fraud, citing the wife's financial manipulations and the children's lack of interest.

The judge ruled: "I cannot set aside this adoption. It was done for the benefit of the children, not the parents."

He then went on to rule that, because the children still see their natural father, *both* men should contribute equally to their support.

The lawyer wanted to appeal, feeling it could be an important test case, but his client was completely out of money and was unable to fight on.

But, the story didn't end there.

The question of the legality of the adoption took place in one Northern California county and the divorce came up in another county. The judge listening to the divorce action was baffled by the adoption resolution and said, "Wait a minute, here. Sharing in child support means there are two legal fathers. This cannot be. Either there is an adoption or there isn't."

So the stepfather, turned adoptive father, reinherited his full child support obligations for the children of the woman who just divorced him, and the natural father was off the hook.

A bizarre tale, but it happened.

In more normal circumstances, where there is no collusion, and when all members of the stepfamily feel it is a wise and healthy move to adopt, the consent of the noncustodial parent is still required along with the consent of the child if he is 12 or over.

We've referred to the noncustodial parent here (rather than father) because there are, of course, circumstances where a stepmother does adopt her husband's offspring even though their mother is alive. This type of adoption does not occur frequently, but when it does it is a symbolic demonstration of an unusual family closeness.

If the biological parent isn't sure whether or not he or she wants to sign the agreement, custody officers are available to help work things out. One official explained, "You never know how these confrontations will finish. I had one case where the stepfather had it all: money, prestige and an affluent life. But he was a cold fish. The real father was a slob, but he was warm and loving, and really didn't know what to do for his daughter's sake. We halted the adoption.

"Then, on the other hand, we had a natural mother who was screwing up the adoption of her four children by their stepmother. She had never been an interested parent and admitted she didn't want the job. The stepmother had virtually raised the kids. The mother really only wanted some attention, so we listened. A lot. Then she agreed to the adoption."

Most stepadoptions, though, involve the man's adopting his wife's children, and in 75 percent of these cases the biological father does give permission. No hassle, no battle.

Why is this parent so agreeable to handing over his issues to another? Nine times out of ten it is because of that old root: money. The natural father may feel his only chance for a life of his own is to get the financial yoke off his back. If he has remarried and begun raising other children, the load may be too great. And for those who never cared for sharing the paycheck in the first place, it is an ideal solution.

As for the remaining reasons for a father's giving up his child or children, it runs about half-and-half for those who don't give a damn and for those who really feel it is better for the child.

One father said: "A kid with two dads gets confused. Money isn't the problem. I've got money. I'm thinking of my boy's welfare."

That type of altruism is rare.

What happens if you can't get the approval of the natural father because you can't find him? That may be a problem but it is, by far, the easiest to solve. The adoption will be delayed but it can proceed without the parent's permission.

The lawyer files a petition, citing abandonment and/or lack of child support, usually after a year's absence. A notice to this effect is published in a newspaper or periodical in order to give the missing parent a chance to reply. If the father can be located but has not payed support, he is served with a citation to appear in court. In either case, the action goes forward.

On the following pages are sample adoption forms.

In a normal adoption the attorney files a petition with the superior court for which a fee of five dollars is charged. Then the department of social welfare is notified. They, in turn, ask the family for all pertinent records: birth and marriage certificates, and divorce papers.

When everything is in order, another meeting with the parents and child is arranged to make sure they are still agreeable. Even at this late date, a child, as well as any of the adults involved, may still have second thoughts about the adoption.

In such an event the proceedings are suspended and often a court psychologist will work with the child to try to get at his inner feelings and determine what the real objection is.

Many times, they say, the problem stems from the youngster's fantasy about his natural parents' getting back together again. The therapist may ask the child to think about those days with his parents: "Were you really happy living with the daily quarrels?"

After the child sees and accepts the truth, he's most likely to let go of his fantasy and start living for the present, which may include a very fortunate adoption.

Once the final decision has been made, there is a waiting period of six months, although this period varies from state to state, and then a brief hearing in the judge's chambers where he grants the adoption.

At this point, the county clerk seals and expunges previous birth and health records of the child under his old name, if the family wishes. A new birth certificate is issued, and from that moment on the child has a fresh identity. Often, however, in adoptions of children 18 or over, they may prefer to retain their original surname. After all, they've lived with it a long time. The court respects their wish.

The total cost for the attorney's fee is around $300, if one can put a price tag on such an exceptional experience.

And it *can* be an exceptional experience in more ways than one.

**Owen:**  *During one of my broadcasts the callers and I got talking about stepadoptions. A woman by the name of Janet phone in. "I was divorced 20 years ago and remarried shortly*

STATE OF CALIFORNIA—HEALTH AND WELFARE AGENCY       DEPARTMENT OF HEALTH

Original for Court Record
Certified Copy for State Department of Health

## In the Superior Court of the State of California
## in and for the County of _____

*In the Matter of the Petition of*

*Consent to Adoption by Parent*
*Retaining Custody*

_____
Petitioner

*I, the undersigned, being the father/mother of* _____ *do*
                                             Name of Minor
*hereby give my full and free consent to the adoption of said child by*

_____, *who is my*
                 Name of Petitioner (Stepparent)

*husband/wife without relinquishing any of my rights, duties or obligations*
*as his/her natural father/mother, and I hereby join in said petition and*
*respectfully request that the prayer thereof be granted.*

*Said child was born on* _____ *in* _____ *and is*
                         Date                   City and State
*the child of* _____ *and* _____.
             Name of Natural Father           Name of Natural Mother

*Date* _____ 19\_\_\_\_\_.

_____
             Signature of Parent

*Signed in the presence of*

_____
*Title:

    *Either the Clerk of the Superior Court or the Probation Officer may witness.
    *This form for use only when person giving consent is husband or wife of petitioner.*
  *Original for court record, certified copy to be sent immediately to State Department of Health, Sacramento*

AD 2 (6/73)

# COURT REPORT OF ADOPTION

**PART I** — The information in this section must be given as it was before adoption. Without this data it may be impossible to prepare an amended certificate of birth for this child.

## FACTS OF BIRTH

1A. NAME OF CHILD—FIRST NAME | 1B. MIDDLE NAME | 1C. LAST NAME

2. SEX | 3. DATE OF BIRTH | 4. NAME OF PHYSICIAN OR OTHER PERSON WHO ATTENDED THIS BIRTH

5A. PLACE OF BIRTH—NAME OF HOSPITAL | 5B. CITY OR TOWN | 5C. STATE OR FOREIGN COUNTRY

## NATURAL PARENTS' DATA

6A. MAIDEN NAME OF MOTHER—FIRST NAME | 6B. MIDDLE NAME | 6C. LAST NAME (MAIDEN SURNAME)

7A. NAME OF FATHER—FIRST NAME | 7B. MIDDLE NAME | 7C. LAST NAME

**PART II** — Adopting parents must furnish the following information concerning themselves as it was at the date of birth of the above child. This information is used in preparation of the amended certificate of birth.

## ADOPTIVE OR NATURAL MOTHER

8A. MAIDEN NAME OF MOTHER—FIRST NAME | 8B. MIDDLE NAME | 8C. LAST NAME (MAIDEN SURNAME) | 9. BIRTHPLACE (STATE OR FOREIGN COUNTRY)

10. DATE OF BIRTH OF MOTHER (ENTER MONTH, DAY, YEAR) | 11. SOCIAL SECURITY NUMBER OF MOTHER | 12. COLOR OR RACE OF MOTHER | 13A. RESIDENCE OF MOTHER—STREET ADDRESS (STREET AND NUMBER. RURAL ADDRESS OR LOCATION)

13B. RESIDENCE OF MOTHER—CITY OR TOWN | 13C. RESIDENCE OF MOTHER—COUNTY | 13D. RESIDENCE OF MOTHER—STATE

## ADOPTIVE OR NATURAL FATHER

14A. NAME OF FATHER—FIRST NAME | 14B. MIDDLE NAME | 14C. LAST NAME | 15. BIRTHPLACE (STATE OR FOREIGN COUNTRY)

16. DATE OF BIRTH OF FATHER (ENTER MONTH, DAY, YEAR) | 17. SOCIAL SECURITY NUMBER OF FATHER | 18. COLOR OR RACE OF FATHER | 19A. PRESENT OR LAST OCCUPATION | 19B. KIND OF INDUSTRY OR BUSINESS

## INSTRUCTIONS TO STATE REGISTRAR

20. DO YOU WANT AN AMENDED BIRTH RECORD PREPARED? (SPECIFY YES OR NO) | 21. DO YOU WANT THE NAME OF THE HOSPITAL OR OTHER FACILITY WHERE BIRTH OCCURRED OMITTED. AS PROVIDED IN SECTION 10433 OF THE HEALTH AND SAFETY CODE. (SPECIFY YES OR NO) | 22. WHEN A CHILD IS ADOPTED BY AN UNMARRIED MAN OR WOMAN. SPECIFY IF THE PARENT REQUESTS THAT THE AMENDED CERTIFICATE REFLECT THE FACT THAT THE ADOPTION WAS A SINGLE PARENT ADOPTION. AS PROVIDED FOR IN SECTION 10433.1 OF THE HEALTH AND SAFETY CODE (SPECIFY YES OR NO)

## VERIFICATION OF PART II

23. SIGNATURE AND MAILING ADDRESS OF PARENT VERIFYING DATA IN PART II

▲

112

| AGENCY OR DEPARTMENT | 24. NAME AND MAILING ADDRESS OF AGENCY OR DEPARTMENT WHICH INVESTIGATED OR HANDLED CASE |
| --- | --- |
| ATTORNEY | 25. NAME AND MAILING ADDRESS OF ATTORNEY |
| PART III | The county clerk should require that as much of the information as is available in Parts I and II, above, be furnished before he completes Part III and forwards the report to the State Registrar of Vital Statistics. |

| 26. I HEREBY CERTIFY THAT THE CHILD DESCRIBED ABOVE WAS ADOPTED BY THE ABOVE NAMED ADOPTIVE PARENT(S) ON THE_____ DAY OF _____ 19___ AS SET FORTH IN THE DECREE OF ADOPTION MADE ON THAT DATE. IN CASE NUMBER _____ | 27. DATE OF FILING OF PETITION |
| --- | --- |
| | 28. THE NAME OF THE CHILD AS SET FORTH IN THE DECREE OF ADOPTION |

COUNTY CLERK

| 29. SIGNATURE AND SEAL OF COUNTY CLERK | BY: | 30. DATE SIGNED | 31. CLERK IN AND FOR THE COUNTY OF |
| --- | --- | --- | --- |
| ▲ | | | |

## MAILING INSTRUCTIONS TO STATE REGISTRAR

For cases in which the petition for adoption was filed on or after January 1, 1972 and the child was born in California or a foreign country, a certified copy of the newly amended birth record will be furnished without additional fee, as provided in Section 10439.5 of the Health and Safety Code. Additional copies may be obtained from the State Registrar of Vital Statistics, 744 P Street, Sacramento, California 95814. The fee is $2.00 for each additional certified copy.

| NAME AND MAILING ADDRESS OF PERSON TO WHOM CERTIFIED COPY IS TO BE SENT | NAME |
| --- | --- |
| | STREET ADDRESS |
| | ADDRESS—CITY OR TOWN. STATE. ZIP CODE |

STATE OF CALIFORNIA. DEPARTMENT OF PUBLIC HEALTH. BUREAU OF VITAL STATISTICS

(REV 1-1-72) FORM VS-44

113

# INSTRUCTIONS

A court report of adoption shall be completed and transmitted to the Office of the State Registrar of Vital Statistics by the county clerk for each decree of adoption granted by any court in the State of California. Court reports of adoption for births which occurred in another state, the District of Columbia, in any territory of the United States, or Canada, shall be transmitted to the appropriate registration authority by the Office of the State Registrar of Vital Statistics.

The information contained in Part I and Part II of this certificate shall be furnished in order to identify and seal the original certificate and prepare an amended certificate. The agency or department handling the case should fill out Parts I and II.

The adoptive parents may request that a new birth certificate not be established by the Office of the State Registrar by entering "No" in Item 20. (Section 10432.1 of the Health and Safety Code)

The adoptive parents may request the Office of the State Registrar to omit the specific name and address of the hospital or other facility where the birth occurred by entering "Yes" in Item 21. (Section 10433 of the Health and Safety Code)

When a child is adopted by an unmarried man or woman the adopting parent may request the Office of the State Registrar to reflect the fact that it is a single-parent adoption on the amended birth certificate by entering "Yes" in Item 22. (Section 10433.1 of the Health and Safety Code)

One of the adopting parents should verify the information in Part II, Items 8 through 22, and sign in Item 23 and also enter their current address. The name and address of the agency or department and the attorney handling the case should be given in Items 24 and 25.

The County Clerk may complete any items in Part I or Part II from the information furnished in the court record.

See reverse side for information on how to apply for a certified copy of an amended birth certificate.

A fee of five dollars ($5.00) shall be paid to the County Clerk at the time of filing the petition in an adoption proceeding for the services required by statute of the Office of the State Registrar. (Section 26860 of the Government Code)

114

For cases in which the petition for adoption was filed on or after January 1, 1972, and the child was born in California or a foreign country, a certified copy of the newly amended birth record will be furnished without additional fee, as provided in Section 10439.5 of the Health and Safety Code. Additional copies may be obtained from the State Registrar of Vital Statistics, 744 P Street, Sacramento, California 95814. The fee is two dollars ($2.00) for each additional certified copy.

Where to write for certified copies of amended birth records if the birth did not occur in California or a foreign country.

If the birth occurred in another state, District of Columbia, in a territory of the United States, or Canada, a certified copy of the amended record may be obtained by writing to the "Registrar of Vital Statistics" at the appropriate address below:

ALABAMA. MONTGOMERY. 36104
ALASKA. JUNEAU. 99801
AMERICAN SAMOA. PAGO PAGO. 96920
ARIZONA. PHOENIX. 85009
ARKANSAS. LITTLE ROCK. 72201
CANAL ZONE. BALBOA HEIGHTS
COLORADO. DENVER. 80220
CONNECTICUT. HARTFORD. 06115
DELAWARE. DOVER. 19901
DISTRICT OF COLUMBIA. WASHINGTON. D.C.. 20001
FLORIDA. JACKSONVILLE. 32201
GEORGIA. ATLANTA. 30303
GUAM. AGANA. 96910
HAWAII. HONOLULU. 96801
IDAHO. BOISE. 83701
ILLINOIS. SPRINGFIELD. 62706
INDIANA. INDIANAPOLIS. 46207
IOWA. DES MOINES. 50319
KANSAS. TOPEKA. 66612
KENTUCKY. FRANKFORT. 40601
LOUISIANA. NEW ORLEANS. 70160
MAINE. AUGUSTA. 04330
MARYLAND. BALTIMORE. 21201
MASSACHUSETTS. BOSTON. 02133
MICHIGAN. LANSING. 48914
MINNESOTA. ST. PAUL. 55101
MISSISSIPPI. JACKSON. 39205

MISSOURI. JEFFERSON CITY. 65102
MONTANA. HELENA. 59601
NEBRASKA. LINCOLN. 68509
NEVADA. CARSON CITY. 89701
NEW HAMPSHIRE. CONCORD. 03301
NEW JERSEY. TRENTON. 08625
NEW MEXICO. SANTA FE. 87501
NEW YORK (EXCEPT NEW YORK CITY)
ALBANY. 12208
NEW YORK CITY
BRONX BOROUGH. 10457
BROOKLYN BOROUGH. 11201
MANHATTAN BOROUGH. 10013
QUEENS BOROUGH. JAMAICA. 11432
RICHMOND BOROUGH. STATEN ISLAND. 10301
NORTH CAROLINA. RALEIGH. 27602
NORTH DAKOTA. BISMARCK. 58501
OHIO. CO:UMBUS. 43215
OKLAHOMA. OKLAHOMA CITY. 73105
OREGON. PORTLAND. 97207
PENNSYLVANIA. HARRISBURG. 17120
PUERTO RICO. SAN JUAN. 00908
RHODE ISLAND. PROVIDENCE. 02903
SOUTH CAROLINA. COLUMBIA. 29201
SOUTH DAKOTA. PIERRE. 57501
TENNESSEE. NASHVILLE. 37219
TEXAS. ALSTIN. 78701

TRUST TERRITORY OF THE PACIFIC ISLANDS
SAIPAN. MARIANA ISLANDS. 96950
UTAH. SALT LAKE CITY. 84113
VERMONT. BURLINGTON. 05402
VIRGINIA. RICHMOND. 23220
VIRGIN ISLANDS (U.S.)
ST. THOMAS. 00802
ST. CROIX
WASHINGTON. OLYMPIA. 98502
WEST VIRGINIA. CHARLESTON. 25311
WISCONSIN. MADISON. 53702
WYOMING. CHEYENNE. 82001

CANADA
ALBERTA. EDMONTON
BRITISH COLUMBIA. VICTORIA
MANITOBA. WINNIPEG
NEW BRUNSWICK. FREDERICTON
NEWFOUNDLAND. ST. JOHN
NOVA SCOTIA. HALIFAX
ONTARIO. TORONTO
PRINCE EDWARD ISLAND. CHARLOTTETOWN
QUEBEC
SASKATCHEWAN. REGINA
YUKON TERRITORY AND THE NORTH WEST
TERRITORIES. DEPARTMENT OF NORTH-ERN AFFAIRS.
OTTAWA

*after. My husband adopted my two children, and they were thrilled to have a father. Three years later we had a child of our own. **Our** daughter is 16 now, and just doesn't get along with her dad at all. I guess they are too much of the same temperament. But our older two, the original stepchildren, realize what this man has done for them and they love him dearly."*

You never know do you? The two older girls appreciate their relationship with their father because they know what it's like *not* to have it. So often, natural children obscure the value of having both loving parents in the home because of personality clashes when the misunderstanding might be cleared up with some honest and understanding communication.

**Nancie:** *Some couples see adoption as the only equitable solution while others never even considered it. We fit into the latter category.*

*Owen has never thought about giving up his fatherly responsibilities although he has been separated by distance from his children most of their lives. The relationships have been less than perfect through lack of proximity, but the children have always had a strong image of him. And particularly since he and I have been married, the three of them have known that our home is their home whenever they want it to be.*

*The fact that David, the eldest, chose to live near us for awhile indicates there is a loving attachment for his father that he wants to maintain. He enjoys being with us. We feel that, although I think he is a bit amused by our behavior, as well. I've never been quite certain if it's because he thinks we're unorthodox or completely square! Nevertheless, we have really good times together. There was just one problem. We didn't know exactly where David lived when he was here. Respecting a child's independence is one thing but how would you like to address your son's mail to a post office box number two miles away? David, where were you?*

*As I said before, with Richard we have had less involvement, unfortunately. But since his and Sally's vacation with us and one other visit he made with David, we are making headway.*

*As for Ellen, as soon as we had a judge determine our visitation rights hour by hour, we were able to build a stable, loving relationship. She is close to Owen in ways only a little girl knows about, and she refers to me as her "other mother." Now, at eleven, she has moved to Southern California, and we're seeing her even more often.*

*My children have a father who definitely wants a place in their lives, as Owen does with his gang, so we have respected his position and kept his image intact all along the line. I keep him well informed on their lives and he sees them whenever he chooses, without conditions, as we all strive to do what's in the interest of the children. They have responded by loving us all equally.*

*It has not always been ideal with either ex-spouse, I must say. And, I'm sure, they feel the same way about us. We've been annoyed, we've been inconvenienced, we've been angered, but we have accepted the drawbacks as part of stepfamily life, without getting overly dramatic. Frankly, even with the conflicts we've had, Owen and I have been able to provide a home for all the children—his and mine—that reflects the love we have for each other. Our house may be a turnstile with kids packing and unpacking, coming and going; but we hope that, in the long run, we have not confused them, but have instead contributed to their expansion and development.*

**Owen:** *Although this has been our way, there is also the stepparent who doesn't want to adopt but does wish to have some authority. This possibility was explored by a radio caller one morning when I was discussing legalities with Arden Weinberg.*

**Caller:**     I'm 35. I've married this gal with a 10-year-old son. And although the father has flown the coop, I'm not sure I want to adopt the boy. You see, I'm also a stepchild and I have many questions in my mind as to whether I should ask this boy to take my name. But what worries me is, suppose my wife is away and the child is injured at school? As it stands now, I don't have the legal right to pick him up and have him admitted to a hospital. Is there a way I can become his legal guardian?

**Attorney Weinberg:**     Yes, of course. Adoption means a change to a permanent relationship, personally and legally, but a guardianship stops just short of that. A guardian does not have the same legal responsibilities nor the same obligations to support the child. But a guardian is a person in charge of bringing up the child.

If you want to be appointed guardian, fine, but you don't really need that to handle those emergencies you were talking about. A simple note from the mother stating that she is giving you the right to act on her behalf is all you need. She can make sure the school and the doctor have the same written permission. That's all that's necessary.

We have not actually come across a family who has implemented this solution, but we did learn about a couple who compromised in a far more unique way.

The stepfather adopted his wife's young children and they chose to take his name. But the couple recognized that there was a need for the boy and girl to stay in touch with the biological father.

Here's how they worked it out.

Every summer, the natural father takes the kids for the entire vacation period. He supports them for the three months and buys them school clothes before returning them in September.

When we asked the couple how they accomplished this incredibly mature arrangement, the mother responded with candor: "It wasn't easy. We were just as mixed up as everybody else. It took two years of constant communication. In the beginning there were so many resentments I didn't think we'd ever get it straightened out."

Then she smiled and added, "But now everybody wins. The children and their father aren't cut off, and my husband and I have our summers free — to do as we please."

Why does a stepfather adopt?

We asked this stepfather just that.

"The decision was made for me when the kids one day told me that if ever they were sick or got injured they wanted *me* to stay with them. That did it."

And that says it all, doesn't it?

# The Beardsleys Revisited

Without a doubt, the most famous stepfamily of the twentieth century would have to be Frank and Helen Beardsley, who were married way back in 1961 and merged 18 children, later to grow to 20 when they had two of their own.

Helen's first husband, a Navy flier, had been killed in an air crash, while Frank's wife died suddenly of diabetes, leaving Frank with 10 children, including a six-month old baby. Helen had 8.

Their marriage caused worldwide interest as they started their new lives together on the Monterey Peninsula.

Helen wrote of their early days in her book, *Who Gets the Drumstick*. And later Lucille Ball produced a movie called "Yours, Mine, and Ours" in which she played the part of Helen Beardsley.

How goes it with the Beardsleys some 15 years later, now that they're no longer famous? They never were rich.

**Owen:** *As I talked to them both on the air and at lunch, I found that many of the things Nancie and I had stumbled onto in becoming stepparents the Beardsleys had found out long ago.*

**Owen:**   Frank, what were the first few months like? You're an old Navy guy. Suddenly, you had a household with 18 children, which is absolutely ridiculous. Did you post a bulletin board with: "Now hear this. This is the uniform of the day?"

**Frank:**   A lot of people think like you did—mass confusion. But I had already organized things pretty well. I had added onto our house so that we had eight bedrooms, five baths, and two family rooms. And then Helen brought a well-organized family, too. But still, I probably did use the Navy way of doing things a little. I organized a kitchen detail, a laundry room detail, and a dishes detail. We had "a, b, and c teams.

**Owen:**   Any griping in the early days?

**Frank:**   Not really. It was completely the opposite of some of the things you saw in the movie. I mean, our house was on three levels and that helped us in the separation of the boys and the girls.

**Owen:**   So you didn't separate by families?

**Frank:**   Oh, no, boys and girls, that was the only way.

**Owen:**   Did everybody have a job?

**Frank:**   Everybody. And that became a problem. We had so many pairs of hands that we didn't have enough jobs around the house to keep them all busy.

**Helen:**   We had more people than we needed, even built-in baby-sitters. So Frank and I were able to take weekends off—something we'd never been able to do before.

**Owen:**   Did the older kids complain?

**Frank:**   Not really. Everybody had a responsibility, and nobody was able to get away with anything.

|            | Everybody was watching somebody else. We had a ready-made honor system. |
|------------|---|
| **Owen:**  | How many are left in the household today? |
| **Helen:** | There are six, soon to be five, with two graduating from high school. And they're ready to be on their own, probably more ready than youngsters from the so-called more normal households, because of the responsibilities they've had. |
| **Owen:**  | Where are the older ones today? What's happened to the Beardsleys? |
| **Helen:** | Well, Michael's a CPA. Rusty is a detail representative for a pharmaceutical company. Gregory has graduated from college in real estate. Rosemary works in a stock brokerage office. We have four who are married, three in college, and we have six grandchildren already. |
| **Owen:**  | How were you able to swing this financially, putting that mass of bodies through college? |
| **Helen:** | They put themselves through. Sure, we did have some help from the VA, but it was up to each child to figure out how. The one thing we stress in our family is that you have to have a skill. You have to be able to support yourself. And if you want to go to college, you better make sure you're going into something that's going to pay off. Philosophy and dreaming, forget it! It has to be productive. Now all our kids haven't wanted college, but they all have a skill, and that's the important thing. |
| **Owen:**  | I still can't get over 20 children! If your house is like ours, and each kid has friends of his own and they all have guests over, did you ever find yourself walking around your own house wondering "Who *are* those strange little faces?" |

**Helen:** (laughing) Frank came up the stairs one day, looking a bit unhappy. We have a pool table down in the rec room, and he said, "You know, there are nine kids down there, and not one of them is a Beardsley."

**Frank:** Everyone wants to be around where there are children; the more the merrier. And yet they want to be in a home where there is supervision, where there are rules and regulations. Children like a situation that is reasonably structured.

**Owen:** After you two had your own children, what was the reaction from the other kids?

**Helen:** They loved it. It was kind of a solidifying thing. Our children are very warm and very outgoing and very unselfish. So the idea of two more kids, they thought it was real fun. And both of *our* kids have been the apples of all the others' eyes.

**Owen:** In the early days, when your family was surrounded by all that publicity, did it affect the children?

**Helen:** Frank would put them straight on that. Sure, a couple of them got big heads. But then I'd say, "Just remember, without the other 19, you're nobody."

**Owen:** Frank, did you adopt Helen's children?

**Frank:** Yes, we both did. We adopted each other's children just a couple of years after we were married.

**Owen:** Helen, why would *you* bother to adopt Frank's?

**Helen:** Well, suppose something happened to Frank? A wife is not necessarily the legal guardian of her own children in some states. So it's just a wise thing to do. And then there is the emotional side. It really is the final commitment.

That word "commitment" is bandied about, but it lets the kids know you really care, and that you really want them. It makes the whole thing official, and it's important to them.

**Owen:** How did you swing the financial part of adopting 18 children? An attorney can charge you $300 each. Did you get a package deal?

**Helen:** Exactly. In fact, better than a package deal. We have a dear friend who's a municipal judge in San Francisco. He didn't charge us a penny. He made us an offer we couldn't turn down.

**Owen:** We've run into other families who tried to merge families with disastrous results. Each child tried to look to his own parent when a problem came up. How did you handle this?

**Helen:** Well, it all should start with your own children, long before a second marriage, and how well you've raised them. But once you do remarry, those new parents have to stick together. They cannot allow themselves to be used, one against the other, and it will happen in any family. Maybe there's a situation where I don't agree with Frank. But it's suicide to let the children know that at that moment. You can't iron it out in front of them. I might try to smooth it over a bit, and then say something later, on the side. If your kids know they have you in conflict, they've won the battle right there.

**Owen:** Then I'm doubly amazed that you two were able to make it.

**Helen:** Our children wanted this to work so much, and they worked so hard at it, that by the time they relaxed, we were already one family.

**Owen:** How well did the two sets of kids know each other before you got married?

**Helen:** Not well at all. Consequently, they did what husbands and wives first do. They had their best foot forward: "I can work as hard as you can; I can be as nice as you can." And, therefore, they jelled, because everybody was trying. And remember, we had one big advantage. Unlike a new marriage from a divorce situation with the natural parents still around, our kids had nowhere else to go. Sure they tried harder.

**Owen:** What are holidays like at the Beardsleys? Does everyone come back to the nest?

**Helen:** Last Thanksgiving, we've been laughing about this, we had 36 for dinner. Between the married ones and the girl friends and boy friends, it was really wonderful. We have a family room that's 43 feet long, so we put a big banquet table down the middle and just had a ball. Holidays are wonderful at our house.

**Frank:** But it's not just at holidays. Our kids keep coming back in droves. I tell you, we'd love to sell our house, buy a one-bedroom place somewhere, and put up a big sign that says "No Room at the Inn."

**Owen:** What if you had it to do all over again, raising 20 children with today's cost of living?

**Helen:** If you really want to bring the phrase cost of living to terms that everybody can understand, it now costs me the same to feed eight children as it used to cost to feed 20. I couldn't do it today.

**Owen:** Did you ever have any problems with your kids into booze or dope?

**Helen:** We had one girl, who was still in high school, I don't know what she was trying to prove.

Someone brought her two bottles of Cold Duck. She got so sick. Next morning, she didn't want to go to school. You can imagine how Frank reacted to that.

**Frank:**   I told her. If you can handle the Cold Duck, you can handle school. I don't care how bad you feel.

**Owen:**   In the early days of your marriage, did either of you have qualms about disciplining the other's children? Here were kids whom each of you really didn't know. How did you handle it in the beginning?

**Frank:**   Sure, there were qualms. If it were one of mine, I wouldn't think twice if I had to belt him. But I purposely would never lay a hand on one of hers if I could help it.

**Helen:**   I think we were both pretty cautious at first. I think we both found ourselves leaning over backward for the other's children, maybe to the detriment of our own. But I don't think it took us too long before our premise was: "Look, we're here because we love each other. And if I sound mean, you must remember I really do love you. It's because I love you that I have to tell you this."

**Owen:**   But *did* you love them at first? You didn't even know these new little people?

**Helen:**   No, I didn't love them. And most of them you don't really ever love the way you love your own. And, yet actually I get along with some of Frank's children better than with some of my own.

**Owen:**   But still, there is the point where every stepparent says, "I really *love* these kids"? Or is that point ever reached?

**Helen:** I don't think that point ever has to be reached. I don't think it's that important. You do get to the point where you really care. Let's not get so-called love and really caring mixed up. Let's not define these terms too closely, because I don't think it's all that important. Look, we do our best. We try to communicate with our kids. And I think that's what is important.

**Owen:** Frank, what about you? I'm sure you were going through the same qualms as Helen, plus you had the added burden of supporting all these people?

**Frank:** That's right. But, if you really love this person, you're going to do everything in your power to make things go. I didn't look at this whole thing as a dollar drain. It was a union, and now they're my children.

**Owen:** In the beginning everyone thought you'd have no financial problems, that advertising agencies would flood you with requests for endorsements, that you'd be on easy street.

**Helen:** We did a series of commercials for a bread company. But the other so-called deals? You wouldn't believe them. One company that manufactures blue jeans said: "Bring all the kids up to San Francisco. We'll have them all pose in our jeans, and they'll get to keep their pants." Big deal! Get 20 kids all dressed up, take them on a 400-mile round trip, for a pair of jeans? That's the kind of "deals" we were offered.

**Frank:** We never really made any money at all. But at the same time, we didn't want our kids to grow up in a fishbowl either.

**Helen:** Even the movie on our life. Lucille Ball made considerably more than we did. We made

$30,000 over a five-year period, and that didn't keep us going very long.

**Frank:** But look, it came at a time when we were working our tails off and we were in some real financial trouble, so it came in handy, whatever it was.

**Owen:** How did you handle money within your household?

**Helen:** First, the kids were great. They made it happen. They simply did without a lot of material things that their friends had. Even today, they're all working. All the kids have jobs. By 12, all the boys had paper routes, and all the girls were baby-sitting.

**Owen:** Do they contribute any of their money to the household?

**Frank:** One-fourth of everything they make. That's always been the rule. They make four dollars, they give me one.

**Owen:** How did you handle television with 20 children watching?

**Helen:** We were quite severe about TV, because we don't think it's good for them. So there was no TV on school nights at all. They could watch it after school on Fridays and until 9 P.M. on Sundays. Then, during the summer, there was no TV until after 4 P.M. During the days they had to get out and play tennis and exercise.

**Owen:** With 20 kids, who decided what to watch?

**Frank:** No problem. The majority ruled.

**Owen:** How important has religion been in your family?

**Helen:** Very important. The children all went to Parochial school and to church on Sundays.

**Owen:** How would you get 20 kids all ready for church at the same time?

**Helen:** We never went to the same Mass. We didn't want to make a spectacle out of ourselves walking in together.

**Owen:** Well, you must see some of these newer step-marriages where there are two sets of children and two different religions. Often religion is taking a back seat.

**Helen:** And I can't agree. I think it's just as important. It's better if the wife goes off to church with her kids, and the husband with his, than not to go at all!

**Owen:** Did you ever take all the kids together anywhere at the same time?

**Frank:** Once, we did take them all to Disneyland. We were having breakfast at the Disneyland Hotel, all of us. People kept staring. Finally, one lady couldn't stand it any longer. She came over to the table and said: "Look, we have a big bet going on over at our table. What is this?" She couldn't believe it was one family.

**Helen:** Of course, now that most of our children have fled the nest, we've noticed a whole new situation taking place. All of our children are friends, mine, his, and ours. But when we do get together or visit one another on occasions, the original families tend now to seek out their own. Yet they're all friends, and they all do care about each other.

**Owen:** Was it always this way with you?

**Helen:** That was my big question when we first married: Do I have enough love to spread? Do I have enough to go around? And I found I did. I told each of them: "If you have a problem, if you want to talk to me alone, I'll make time." And it worked. I was always available,

and I was willing to listen. Through listening
and through communication, comes love and
understanding.

**Frank:**   The other important rule we learned: Never
argue in front of the children. Always support
one another at that moment, even if you think
your spouse is wrong. Then talk about it later.

**Helen:**   I guess this would be even more important in a
stepfamily involving a couple of previous divorces. The kids have already been through
one battle scene. Don't make them think: "Oh,
here we go again."

So, what can we learn from the nation's most successful
stepparents? Pretty much a reinforcement of many of the
things we've already discussed: love, understanding, communication, support of one another, rules, discipline, and
fairness.

Although Helen and Frank do admit that stepparenthood,
without the pressure from previous spouses, did give them a
much stronger start: "Our kids tried harder. Our family was
all they had."

But Frank and Helen, you're wrong. Your kids tried harder
because you offered the best home in town!

# Good Grief! I'm a Stepparent!

If Helen and Frank Beardsley laid a guilt trip on you with their complete determination and full-time devotion in raising their respective broods, fret not.

That's one viewpoint. But not everyone feels that way. There are those who meet in the middle years, fall in love, and want to spend the rest of their lives together—alone, not necessarily with the parcel of people who come along. Oh, they'll do their best to be friendly to the offspring, but they figure this may be their last chance for happiness, and *they* come first. Actually, it may not be that big a problem, as, often, the kids involved are in their late teens or early twenties and are already off doing their own things.

But, it still came as a bit of a shock when a friend (and new stepparent) told us recently: "I have never been especially fond of children. I really haven't. I adore my own kids, but I'm not a children lover."

So, what's shocking? It wasn't the statement per se. It was the source. Good old Charlie Brown himself. Creator of Linus, the hated Red Baron, the kite-eating tree, Woodstock, and all the "Peanuts" gang, Charles M. Schulz, the world's most famous cartoonist.

131

**Nancie:**   *I couldn't believe what I was hearing! I calculated we'd spent enough money on Snoopy radios, Snoopy sleeping bags, stuffed Snoopys, pencil-sharpening Snoopys, erasing Snoopys, and cookie-cutting Snoopys to furnish an entire room in Sparky Schulz's house. Somehow I imagined it to be a playroom—for children.*

**Owen:**   *But the confusion didn't end there because I had just spent an hour on the air with Sparky, talking about his 25 years of drawing the strip. I had heard him talk with warmth and kindness to a junior high school journalism class on how to get started in cartooning. I watched him take the time to draw and autograph Snoopys for the children of the KGO staff. From a caller I learned of the great interest he has in referreing kids' hockey games at his Ice Arena in Santa Rosa. If Charles M. Schulz doesn't like children, I'm Adolph Hitler.*

Sparky and Jeanie Schulz are simply being honest. They've been married for two years. He inherited her two children; she inherited his five. With the ages ranging from 15 to 23, the kids can pretty much fend for themselves, leaving time for the marriage to develop.

"Our commitment is to each other," they agreed, with Jeanie adding: "We don't really live like a family. We tried it at first, but after all, the kids are older. They go their separate ways. We're living a compromise and our children are, too. They know things could explode if we all got too close, so the stepkids ignore each other."

Isn't this the story in many non-stepfamilies today? Teenagers having these same feelings for their natural siblings and parents experimenting with their roles?

**Jeanie:**   I don't consider myself a stepparent. I'm just somebody who is in the house. That sounds like I'm putting myself down, but I don't mean it that way. I just think I'm somebody married to their father. They're too old for me to try to tell them what to do.

Sparky: And I don't have to be a father to Jeanie's kids. I'm there and I try to help, but I don't have to be a father. And I don't cross her children in any way.

Owen: What happens if one of Jeanie's children makes you absolutely furious?

Jeanie: No one ever does anything that makes Sparky absolutely furious.

This conversation took place over lunch in one of San Francisco's super Chinese restaurants. As the fortune cookies were served after the meal, we couldn't help but wonder what Charles M. Schulz's fortune would be. Would it be a message of defeat, fulfilling the image of Charlie Brown?

The three of us read ours and then watched Sparky as he opened his.

Owen: If this is a loser, I'll die.

Jeanie: They never write losers in these cookies.

Sparky: It says "Your determination will make you succeed." We sighed with relief.

Sparky: But it was torn when I opened it.

# Religion and Realistic Rearing

One of us is a Jew. The other a Christian. There is a picture of us on the dust jacket. Can you tell which is which? Do you really care? Is it worth caring about?

We respect each other's beliefs. We celebrate all pertinent holidays and consider our children damn lucky to be exposed to the education.

**Owen:** *Now you know who's who, but I've got to tell you I make out like a bandit during the eight nights of Hanukkah. Last year, I received eight back rubs from Peter the Great and eight grass cuttings by Chris the Cool. I was trying to get Ashley to promise me eight days of silence, but I settled for an original poem and was proud to get that.*

*At Easter, guess who hides the colored eggs for the kids? Me. And what a job I've done. There are now four eggs somewhere in our yard that have remained undiscovered since 1973.*

To us, getting uptight about a difference in religion is like fretting over one partner's preferring crunchy peanut butter to the smooth blend. After all, they both come from the same nut.

We recognize, however, that there are couples who might consider religion an issue in stepparenting. So, we looked into the matter for our edification as well.

Interviewing a divorced Episcopal minister, who is raising two stepchildren and fighting for custody of his own three children, seemed a good way to begin.

Because his legal battle is still very much up in the air, we'll call him Alex and his present wife, Claire.

Alex had been the number two man at a posh parish in California and was slated for the top slot at an even posher place. He was young, tall, and handsome with a charming style about him. Then, divorce — that terrible scourge — marked the end of his climb.

Today, married to Claire, a natural blonde with a direct approach to things, he is alive and well in a small, far less affluent parish. Actually, it's more like a neighborhood commune. Most informal. No more "I'll preach to you and you sit in the pews and listen." At his new mission, Alex calls everybody a minister. He learns as much from them as they from him.

Has Alex been criticized by any of his parishioners for his "sordid" past?

"Just because a man turns his collar around doesn't mean he's turned his pants around. No. The people in my congregation have more love and understanding than that. Criticism is beneath them. And, perhaps, some of them derive comfort from the fact that I can see their problems subjectively, since we have a lot of new stepfamilies coming to church."

He went on to comment that he wasn't seeing much trouble in the area of religion and stepparenting: "Even in the case of Roman Catholics and Jews marrying, who, incidentally, seem to attract each other, I see no real problem. Everyone seems to be loosening up both for themselves and for their kids."

Claire added, "There's a feeling today that parents don't want doctrine taught. They prefer for the children to learn *values* in the church schools. One woman told me, 'I've changed ideas so often that things I believed in five years ago, I don't believe anymore. So why should I have to unprogram my kids everytime I switch?'"

What *is* religion to Alex? "I'd define it as a belief in some kind of an ultimate concern. Your religion can be your car, your football team, or your God. I think the best thing stepparents can do for their children is to love each other, rather than worry about how to worship."

Are their children religious? Both Alex and Claire thought about that question for quite some time.

Then Alex answered, "Not really. We do say grace at the table but we don't talk religion in the sense of labeling it. We try to work together and help one another more as a family."

**Nancie:**   *This couple was so warm and real I was bursting to ask them about their personal life. How human are you? Do you swear or smoke or drink or talk about sex, like the rest of us?*

They both laughed.

Alex replied, "We have a cocktail before dinner every night and maybe a little wine, sure."

Claire wanted to take a crack at the swearing. "Alex's children had really been given a free hand in their language when they lived with their mother, and I put up with a lot in the beginning. But I felt it had to stop with 'motherfucker.'"

Alex and Claire are going through serious difficulties right now. Alex's former wife, Sharon, who was tired of mothering after the divorce, has reappeared to try to woo away the children from their father. Her weapon is money. And, apparently, she is succeeding.

Originally, Sharon obtained legal custody of the children but left them with Alex so she could travel after she struck it rich through an inheritance. Now she has returned with a playboy husband and is trying to buy her way back in. She's rented a sumptuous penthouse with fancy gadgets near the solid and immaculate old house where Alex and Claire live. And she's laying on the glamour.

Alex explained, "We're in a real mess, and frankly, my formal religious background isn't helping me that much to get through all of this. What is helping is the love and support from the parish. People are praying for us and crying for us. This is true Christianity at work. But I've got to admit I'm bitter about my kids. They're allowing themselves to be bought. Offer a child a plate of spinach or a Hostess Twinkie and guess which he's going to take?"

"Sharon thinks she wants to play momma again, and she has the bank account to buy her way through the courts," added Claire. Alex's kids have always called me Claire, but yesterday I heard one of them refer to me as her 'stepmother.' I think she's trying to divorce me."

In talking further with this distraught couple we tried to get back to the disadvantages of mixing religions in step-marriages.

Their feelings are that if two people are firmly entrenched in diametrically opposing beliefs, chances are they would never get to the stage where they would consider marriage.

The real problem, then, seems to be with personalities, not principles.

However, there's always an exception.

Child psychiatrist Robert Wald told us about a case where personality and principle did coordinate with deceptive subtlety.

The family, in the story, consists of a Jewish mother and a Catholic father. During the marriage the parents sublimated their religious beliefs with great success. But when they split up, the father returned to Catholicism with fervor.

In treating their five-year-old son, Dr. Wald made this discovery in one of their sessions.

**Child:** "Worry Doctor, I have a new worry."

**Dr. Wald:** "What is it?"

**Child:** "Jessie in Kindergarten is teasing me. He called me a wet potato bug."

**Dr. Wald:** "That's really too bad. Being teased is a worry."

**Child:** "That wasn't the worry. The worry was the stupid teacher caught me when I hit Jessie."

**Dr. Wald:** "That must have been a real pain in the neck."

**Child:** "No. That's a pain in the ear because it means being scolded. The pain in the neck is my bad dweam every night." I keep dweaming about the big 'D.' "

**Dr. Wald:** "The big 'D'?"

**Child:** "The big 'D' is Dwacula. Dwacula comes every night in my dweams, and he chokes me and he sucks my blood. That's why I love to go over to my daddy's house. He's got those big crosses hanging all around. They scare away the big 'D.' "

# Our Baby?

"Haven't you two done enough?"

That was our then 23-year-old sometime resident and big mouth, David Spann, talking.

Over rare roast beef and hot horseradish we asked the children how they would feel if we had a baby.

We loved each other. We got married for the right reasons, and our life together, with our respective progeny, was hectic but successful. We could imagine the joys of raising a baby in complete harmony and inner security.

We could also imagine the sorrows.

Our older bodies might not produce a healthy infant. We might not have the hours and the energy to give proper attention to a seventh individual. We might not have enough money.

And perhaps we would be exposing this child to the death of his parents before he was mature enough to handle it or, even worse, expose him to our senility.

We examined our motives in the naked light of day rather than during the warm passion of night. Children have a right to be planned and brought forth with logic, not sentimentality.

The dilemma was solved with David's flip wisdom. Yes, we had done enough. Between us we had brought six wrinkled, bawling creatures into the world with the right number of arms and legs and, we hoped, all their marbles. Best to stop while we were behind.

Actually, it's the sick joke of the house that the best our union could produce was the dog, a cockapoo.

**Owen:**   *What a name. I don't even like to say it.*

Because a cockapoo is a ·deliberate blend of poodle and cocker spaniel, we reckoned it was an appropriate animal for a stepfamily to own, although we're still undecided as to whether, physically, our Daisy is not the worst of the two breeds. Her tail is nearly as long as her body, her color ranges from white to black while passing through shades of brown, and her hair is neither straight nor curly: it just hangs there.

**Nancie:**   *Just like mine.*

But she is easy to train — very bright, alert, and willing.

**Children (all together):**   *Just like us.*

Well, you get the idea. And at least we don't have to put her through college.

We have to admit, however, that at dinner the night we asked the children how they felt about our having a baby, there was no opposition to the idea from the younger ones.

The teen-age response was, "It's OK with me. It's your life."

Peter thought it was terrific as long as he didn't have to change any diapers. On the other hand, Ellen thought it would be fun to change diapers providing they were only wet.

Ashley had already slipped away to make a bed in her room for the hypothetical "enfant."

We suspect nearly every newly stepmarried couple has pondered the possibility. "Sure, I thought about it for 30 seconds, once," said one lady.

"We'd love to," said another, "except for two reasons. I've had a hysterectomy and my husband has had a vasectomy."

Dr. Elizabeth Whelan in her book *A Baby—Maybe,* talks about the costs of raising a baby to adulthood in the 1970s. She says figure around $103,000, a staggering amount, particularly if you're supporting children from a previous marriage.

Dr. Whelan urges careful consideration: "Children are not returnable. You can have an ex-wife, ex-husband, ex-job but you cannot have an ex-child."

BUT for those ageless, hearty stepsouls who have chosen to have *their* baby, the positives are extraordinary.

Brenda Maddox, who wrote about her experiences in *The Half-Parent,* expressed it this way: "The two children my husband and I had were an absolute delight to his children. It helped them to think of me as a mother, rather than as some sort of girl who arrived to wash the dishes. We had the fun of waiting for the baby to come. A shared happening that was new to them as well as to me."

When the mother and father each contribute offspring from former unions, there are even more positives on the family tree to consolidate. With a new baby to care for, the children can take part in helping, integrating themselves into a closer, more loving life-style. The stepmother becomes more like their real mother; the stepfather, more like their real father. The birth not only legitimizes the household, it also legitimizes everybody's role within it. And the added attraction is that the baby is a blood relation, a half-brother or half-sister to everyone forever. A really special relationship.

But the pressures of legitimizing the household with this dandy little blood tie should, it would seem, be considered with maturity, not with the childish rebellion we heard from one stepmother. She related how her new spouse had, repeatedly, said no to having a baby of their own because of the mounting burdens he had in raising his and hers. The lady smiled triumphantly as she told us how she managed to change his mind: "I simply said, 'Then you don't love me as much as you did *her* [the former wife].' And he capitulated."

Child psychiatrist Dr. Robert Wald showed us another possible dark side to this brand of baby business: "With parents who have neurotic hang-ups of their own, one might see them lavish all their attention on the new addition, to the detriment of their own children. For example, by having a child, the father tries to prove to his other children that this wife is better than their mother. He shows them what a good father he is with the new baby, as compared to their mother, the bitch. The new mother can do the same thing. 'Watch the perfect mother perform. I was this way with your father, too, but he didn't appreciate me.'"

Therefore, having a baby for the wrong reasons could mean a spoiled child, resentful siblings, and parents with big problems.

But when the family is fundamentally sound, the past lovingly buried, and the present honestly wholesome, the patter of tiny tots can be in the future . . . conceivably.

## POSTSCRIPT

**Nancie:**  *No. No. I'm not pregnant.*

*As a matter of fact, I decided to have my tubes tied instead. Although we discussed it openly with the children, I quietly slipped away for a few hours to have this done while they were in school, but the news got around the community anyway.*

*Ashley's second grade teacher, Barbara Kendall, phoned to tell me that during "Share and Tell," Ashley announced proudly that her mother was having her tubes **tightened.***

*"Not **too** tight, I hope," sympathized Barbara.*

# Grandma Who?

We stepped out of the taxi, having just returned from a two-week trip to Egypt.

The sight of seven unfamiliar bicycles parked in the driveway brought us back to home and reality as fast as the very familiar sound of a ringing phone pierced our ears.

Chris ran out the front door. "Oh, hi, Mom and O. Welcome to the world travelers. Grandma's on the telephone."

"Grandma who?" we asked.

"Grandma Ruth," he answered.

**Owen:** *That's my mother. No relation to the Anderson kids but very much a part of our elongated family and very much an accepted grandma to them as well as her own.*

**Nancie:** *Last spring during Ellen's stay with us, my mother happened to be visiting, too. Early one morning I walked into Nana's room to find her and her stepgranddaughter cuddled in bed together talking in low and intimate tones. Would a stranger to the scene have known they were not related?*

Each year in July and December, we are offered a week's use of the Lake Tahoe home of the senior Andersons. The only stipulation is that we take the grandchildren. They've never said which ones.

Are we lucky in these relationships? Or did we make our luck? Who knows for sure? What we do know, however, is that we all made an effort to get along.

**Nancie:**    *I felt it was my job to get the ball rolling, to keep in touch, reaffirming old ties while establishing new ones.*

*I wrote a sort of letter of introduction to Owen's mother before we were married, explaining who I was as a person, what my goals were in life, and describing the children. Many times she has told me how much she appreciated that letter. And to think I nearly didn't mail it because I was shy and embarrassed!*

*Getting the children to write, too, especially thank you notes, has caused about 90 percent of the wrinkles on my forehead, but it's so important to securing the stepgrandparent relationship that I regret not one of them. My rule is: The letters can be short but they must be done **now.***

*Stepgrandparents need to be remembered and they deserve to be remembered, whether they remember back or not. Surely parents, in general, agree that children should be taught to think of others on birthdays, holidays, and special occasions, so what's wrong with extending that thought to the extended relatives?*

*Mailing a kindergartener's finger painting or a teen-ager's first expression in poetry may not illicit a mention in a step-grandparent's last will and testament, but it might bring a smile to a lonely face.*

*And a greeting card signed by everyone in the household can look a little weary after it's made the rounds for signatures. But what are a few smudges and stains in a stepfamily? Aren't we all smudged and stained by the time we get together, anyway?*

**Owen:** *God knows, we don't make it easy for the older generation. During the period Nancie and I were living together, my mother and stepfather, Joe, and the Andersons were not at all pleased—particularly the Andersons, as we were an embarrassment in their community. My parents, living in the East, didn't have that to face, nor were the grandchildren-theirs; but morally they were definitely against the arrangement.*

**Nancie:** *Yet, these four disapproving parents allowed us to keep the communication going. There were no ultimatums or threats. I think it is fair to say we were considerate of each other out of respect for what was due the grandchildren and for the home that was being created for them.*

*I'll never forget the beautiful gift Alice Anderson gave Chris, Peter, and Ashley when she told them: "I love your Mommy and I always will." These confused children were so relieved to know there was no chasm dividing family loyalties that I never realized how much they had thought about it until then. It was actually a generous show of approval.*

**Owen:** *Approval doesn't end with the kids. Adults need it, too.*

*One of my favorite regular callers on my show, Phil, related his personal story: "My wife has a child by a previous marriage who was quite a handful in the beginning. In fact, she was a brat. I worked with her for months trying to bring some loving discipline into her life, but I really didn't know how I was doing. Then she went to visit her father and the two sets of grandparents during the summer. I received wonderful letters from them all saying how marvelous the change in the child was . . . what a nice person she was to be around . . . not a monster anymore. Without that feedback I probably wouldn't have kept at it, but those letters were, oh, it sounds dumb, an inspiration, but it's true."*

*And Phil is right. It does feel good to know the step-in-laws approve.*

*When Alice and Walter Anderson invited me to dinner along with Nancie and the children, I enjoyed the evening because no one came with any hang-ups or hostilities. We were all quite civilized and relaxed, although I did put my foot down about including their son, Nancie's ex-spouse. He may refer to me as "his husband-in-law," but family togetherness can go just so far.*

We feel pity for the stepparent who told us: "My mother doesn't even know I've remarried, let alone know she has step-grandchildren. She could never accept it."

Who can say what kin will accept when they have no alternative? How many times have we all said we couldn't possibly do something until the moment of truth arrives and we do it?

Of course there are distant grandparents, not only geographically but emotionally, who never cared for the role and never will, no matter whose children are involved. One step-mother we interviewed confirmed this by explaining that her mother wouldn't recognize her stepgrandchildren if she passed them on the street. Nor would she recognize her natural grandchildren, as she hadn't made much effort to see them either.

It was this same attractive, well-educated woman who said, "I think divorce and remarriage is a whole new way of life, and we must reconcile ourselves to the fact that the old family ties are gone."

Perhaps for some families this attitude is the most comfortable way to operate. Obviously, it eliminates problems. Problems to some, however, may translate into loving responsibility for others.

Brenda Maddox, author of *The Half-Parent,* expressed this point of view: "I find the grandparents get much more actively involved with their grandchildren's lives after a divorce. More so than any of us imagine. If given the chance, they can provide a sense of continuity."

Some grandparents have actually gone to great trouble and expense to wage long legal battles to maintain that chance.

Take the case of Mr. and Mrs. Gabriel Vacula of New York State. Their former daughter-in-law was awarded custody of their grandchild in a bitter divorce suit in 1971, during which animosity spread to the grandparents.

In a suit before the New York State Court of Appeals, the Vaculas testified that not only was communication cut off, but that their Christmas and birthday gifts to their granddaughter were returned unopened.

The court eventually ruled that grandparents *are* entitled to visit their grandchildren, even when the family has been broken by divorce, and even if they are on bad terms with the parents.

Isn't it a shame that the Vaculas had to go to such extremes to keep in touch with their very own granddaughter?

This continuity can be extremely valuable with a remarriage and stepchildren. With no one really knowing where or how they belong at the outset, the grandparents and stepgrandparents can well serve as solidifiers, gluing the family together. It would seem like a very rewarding achievement for those who want the experience.

But naturally they must be given the opportunity. Often grandparents have feelings of insecurity and concern when, for instance, the ex-wife of their son marries another man. They can be stricken with worry that they will lose their grandchildren. They can fear the ex-daughter-in-law will change the childrens' names to match the stepfather's, or deny them visiting privileges, or move away completely. These fears are quite real and valid.

Stepgrandparents can be ostracized even easier by simply being ignored by the new children-in-law. They rarely make the first gesture, as they are uncertain of their position and don't want to intrude.

So now we get down to custodial parental responsibility, accepting the rights of *all* grandparents to *be* grandparents. A divorce does not invalidate the role nor should a remarriage inhibit it.

Grandparenthood is not forever. Grandparents die. And in this precarious world, don't we all need each other for as long as we have?

Who cares if its a natural relationship or a hyphenated one. We don't.

**Nancie:**   *Nor does Owen's stepfather, apparently.*

*When Grandpa Joe was out here visiting, he took Ellen, his stepgranddaughter, and Ashley, his stepgranddaughter-in-law, shopping. Actually, the girls maneuvered him into the toy section of our local five-and-ten, but he was a willing soft touch.*

*Subsequently, he allowed each of them to choose a gift. Ashley picked out a doll for $1.98, while Ellen, far more worldly, decided on a $4.95 number.*

*Grandpa interceded, explaining that Ashley could upgrade her purchase to match Ellen's.*

*Watching all this, I whispered to Joe that it was not necessary, that Ashley would not feel slighted, nor did I expect him to even things up. I lectured on about how it was impossible to treat any set of children alike, how it wasn't practical or constructive, because everyone had different needs at different times. Oh, I really talked!*

*When I'd finished, Joe just smiled at me and said, "Today they can be equal."*

# Holidays: Feast or for the Birds?

**Nancie:**   *My ex-husband, Dean, walked into the kitchen one Sunday having just returned Chris and Peter from a bachelor weekend.*

*What are you going to do about Thanksgiving?" he asked.*

*"Well, we were waiting to see what your plans were."*

*"I don't have any plans this year," was his gloomy reply, as he had been recently divorced after a brief second marriage.*

*It turned out that his mother, who was not particularly well, had decided to take the family to the club, rather than prepare a turkey dinner at home.*

*Because the children were not going to miss a festive meal at the paternal parental hearth, I felt it was fair to speak up and ask to have them spend the day with us.*

*After all, they're all the family we have.*

*Ellen, by court edict, spends all important holidays with her mother; and since David couldn't find a legal way to fame and fortune in California, he has returned to Georgia.*

*Obviously, we would dearly love to be able to fly both David and Richard out for these occasions, but until Delta Airlines comes through with a courtesy jet, our budget pales at the cost.*

*So without my children, holidays become empty celebra-*
*tions for Owen and me. But that's our problem, not theirs. In*
*exchange for asking my former husband to let us have the*
*children for Thanksgiving, we gave up making any Christmas*
*plans. The children would be available to their father and his*
*family whenever they wished.*

*Compromise. That's our way of solving the holiday step-*
*family blues. It seems to be reasonably mature and unselfish.*

**Owen:**  *I'll never forget our first Thanksgiving together. We*
*didn't have any of the children with us. And what a "winner"*
*that day turned out to be!*

*We decided to surround ourselves with other gay, happy*
*nonparents and made reservations for a gala feast at the Mark*
*Hopkins.*

*What a complete drag!*

*We were dejected. The other guests were dejected. The*
*waiters were dejected. The turkey was dejected. Even the*
*appropriate white wine had seen better days. Never again.*

*In the future, if we find ourselves in a similar situation, we*
*plan to stay home, dress up as tangerines, and watch "Let's*
*Make a Deal."*

At least our solutions are an improvement over the agonies
we keep hearing from parents in the same footsteps.

"Holidays? I dread them." A nearly universal answer we got
from the noncustodial parents to whom we spoke.

Holidays. A form of blackmail used with precise effective-
ness by former mates to try to manipulate and control ex-
spouses and the children alike.

**Nancie:**  *Is there justice in a judge's acquiescing to a*
*custodial mother who insists on having her child with her every*
*Christmas Eve and Christmas Day, when she isn't even a*
*Christian?*

*A Jewish father can't ask for the eight nights of Hanukkah when his child lives three thousand miles away. The mother gets it all. But what does the child get?*

*That's our situation. My children and I could expose Ellen to Christmas as we celebrate it. Every other year, as we asked for in court, she could enjoy the religious customs of her stepfamily and share in the exchange, as her father does.*

*My children have been given the opportunity to learn about the Jewish holy days. They plan for them. They're enthusiastic about them. And they respect them. They're the winners.*

**Owen:**   *I'm not exactly a loser. I end up with eight nights of gifts at Hanukkah. As a matter of fact, that abundance has not gone unnoticed by Miss Ashley, who has already asked me, "How do you get to be Jewish?"*

# It Ain't Ever Going To Be Perfect

**There's never nobody!**

**Owen:**   Nancie, if we don't get out of this house and get away for a weekend soon, I'm going to climb the wall!"

In the preceding chapter, we went into great detail regarding the problems of gathering everyone together at holiday times, to share the love and warmth of the hearth.

What about the reverse? When you want to just plain dump them?

"Dumping" is a normal experience in the life of all parents, natural or step.

But we "steps" have additional headaches.

You'll soon find that you cannot get rid of everybody, all at the same time. It's impossible.

Consider school vacations, a grand time for your wife's ex-husband to take his kids for a week or two. But that's exactly the time that you inherit yours from your ex-wife. Peace and quiet? Hardly. True, there may be fewer mouths to feed, but there will be mouths, always there to remind you that a home of tranquility will mostly be denied you.

*Nancie's ex, Dean, takes his kids on many a weekend. But never all of them. He might take the two boys one time and Ashley the next, feeling this is the best way to give them quality time.*

*But there's never nobody.*

*"Why not just get a sitter?" you may be asking. Have you checked the going rates lately from the Union of Amalgamated Sitters? Based on current inflation and cost-of-living increases, the going rate for a "live in" 24-hour-a-day bonded sitter can vary from $25 to $65 a day, plus food. Actually, I've been considering quitting broadcasting and becoming a professional nana.*

*"Aha, there are always summer camps," you might interject. True. Not only that, but there are camps with specialized interests for every child: baseball, basketball, horseback riding. But, their sessions never coincide. That great "Camp Director in the Sky" appears to conspire against us.*

*Even that occasional night at home alone somehow never seems to work out. A few weeks ago, it really looked like we would have Saturday night by ourselves. Chris and Peter were set for a skiing trip, and Ashley had been invited to "sleep over." I was busily making plans: a roaring fire, a little wine—the whole "dirty old man" bit.*

*So what happened? That great "Camp Director in the Sky's" step-brother, the "Snow Director," didn't cooperate. The ski trip was called off. Ashley's invitation was canceled.*

*Instead of having nobody, we had our three plus three more guests of Peter's. I snuffed out the candles, put the cork back in the wine, and substituted "hanky panky" for "S.W.A.T."*

*The prospects for this August, though, quickly reinforced my hopes.*

*Nancie announced: "I don't believe it. It appears that no child will be here the first half of August. The boys will be with their Dad, and Ashley is going to camp. This is your chance, Hot Shot."*

*Hot Shot (that's me) quickly grabbed it. I rearranged Ellen's summer visit with us, since she was due to arrive in August.*

*I checked with my friendly travel agent and lined up an idyllic tryst on a tropical island called Oahu.*

*I rushed home with the tickets and a brand new Aloha shirt.*

*Then the phone rang.*

*It was David.*

*"Hi there. I thought I'd fly out to see you folks the first of August. Got any room?"*

*There's never nobody.*

### Who's responsible for what?

**Owen:**  *Earlier, when Dean Anderson and I met for that very civilized luncheon regarding the raising of his children, we both came away feeling we had solved the problems that had existed in the past.*

*But that was yesterday.*

*Today has brought a new obstacle that neither one of us had considered.*

*It all started when Nancie said, "Chris got his driving permit today. And his teacher says he should be practicing."*

*And I said, "So?"*

*And Nancie said, "Well, it's your car he'll be practicing on."*

*To which I replied, "Not without insurance he won't. And that's his father's problem."*

*Nancie, once again, was caught in the middle. She checked with her former mate who, in turn, informed her that he was willing to cover whatever liability insurance might be necessary. But he also felt that, since I had undertaken to be stepfather to his children, it was my obligation to undertake the cost of any additional expenses for collision coverage for my car.*

*This annoyed me. I feel I have assumed enough of the day-to-day expenses involving his children.*

*The car, gasoline, and insurance I provide for Nancie's use goes mostly for transportating his children. The message unit telephone calls to him are paid by me. The utility costs of the house are doubled with three extra pair of hands turning the switches. And now this! Insurance for a 16-year-old driver.*

*Yes, I could have laid this whole trip on him, and more. But I didn't.*

*Before I called Dean back to work out the auto insurance deal rationally, I checked with my own agent and got another shock: "Mr. Spann, Chris's father can't insure his son at all even if he wants to. Chris lives in your household and will be driving your car. You are liable, not his father."*

*I was stunned. Have you checked the cost of insuring a new teen-age driver lately? In my case an additional $650 premium notice will be forthcoming. Our total coverage cost will soon resemble the national debt.*

*And I have two more of what's her name's hot-rodders standing in the garage. Waiting. For wheels.*

*Anyhow, I think we've solved it. I took Nancie out of the middle and talked to Dean. He has agreed to cover three-fifths of the liability premium on my policy (and not many fathers would do that) while Chris will kick in with two-fifths from his job at the car wash.*

*Now, if I can just get to Chris first on his paydays, before he gets to the neighborhood taco stand and record store, it'll all work out fine.*

### Who do I turn to?

**Owen:** *Jesus! How can three children use so much water and still look so dirty?*

**Nancie:**   *That was Owen opening the latest monthly state-ments. Our water consumption had doubled.*

*When Chris explained that the reason he stayed in the shower so long was to wake up in the morning, Owen strongly suggested, "Wake up* before *you go into the bathroom."*

*Listening to Harrassed Harry ranting about the high cost of* not *supporting my children led me to a terrible daydream: I die and Chris, Peter, and Ashley choose to live with their stepfather O. The poor stepfather who longs for the days he can be* alone *with his wife buries her and ends up with her children.*

*Diabolical humor aside, there are occasions in stepmar-riages when plans don't turn out storybook fashion. It's when we expect them to that things get out of hand. That's where flexibility becomes an asset.*

*Take pride. Parents are proud of their own children's accomplishments: it comes along with the placenta, I think. But what about the reluctant stepparent? Where are his thoughts?*

*Eleven-year-old blue eyes comes home with straight A's and a 97 percent average. Mother is proud.*

*Baby girl makes an astute comment to the green grocer. Mother is proud.*

*Mister teenage terror rewires the stereo system and saves a repair bill. Mother is proud.*

*But where is stepdaddy's pride? Should these moments of braggadocio be shared with him when nearly every child is bright, funny, clever, and successful at one point or another? Particularly his own.*

*Of course these accomplishments should be shared— children need the reinforcement and parents need to be proud —but with whom? I really had to ask myself that question.*

*Should I bore this husband of mine with these very personal, banal deeds when he's already occupied with his own* kids' achievements; or should I relate them to my children's father who has a real interest and enjoys hearing anecdotes about them?

The answer, for me, was to share with both men.

Feeling comfortable in these circumstances takes developing, but what a great sense of inner security when you reach that level! The inner security that anything goes binds a step-marriage like nothing else. To be open with one's spouse and share the boring and the bragging shows confidence and trust in the relationship. And to be open with an ex-spouse without rancor, exaggeration, or flirtatious inuendo shows the past is past and jealousy has been expurgated from the soul.

This works in reverse, too, when a child gets into trouble. Trouble seems to surface faster than a good performance so all the more reason to share it quickly with both men, then solve it jointly. A parent who protects a child's image by hiding little faults and failings only encourages devious behavior and plays a one-sided game with the stepfather who does the raising and the biological father who does the paying.

### Where did my mistress go?

**Owen:** *"It's still the same old story, a fight for love and glory . . . "*

The same old story?

Man meets girl. Man courts girl. Man sleeps with girl. Everything is perfect. Then man marries girl. Man accumulates debts, a mortgage, and children.

Girl now becomes chief cook and bottle washer, chauffeur, amateur doctor, shopper, maid, and jill of all trades but mistress of nobody.

Life becomes too busy and complex for candlelight, wine, and massages.

*Actually, this is the normal path that most marriages follow. By "normal" I mean first marriages, original marriages, virginal marriages, church marriages.*

*Now, let's talk about stepmarriages.*

*If that first husband suddenly wonders, about 10 years later, where his mistress went, the stephusband doesn't have to wait nearly that long. With the instant family he's inherited, the truth hits home much faster.*

*Sure, in the early days of our marriage Nancie bent over backward to make me "numero uno" in our household, but the children did suffer. Now, she's had to put her priorities in order.*

***Example:** Come Monday mornings she slips into her driving gloves and goggles and steps into her Capri, never to emerge again until Friday afternoons.*

*If it isn't carpool or tutoring or French lessons or the 50-mile drive to Dad's house, it's Ashley's horseback riding or Peter's football games. If it isn't a visit to the orthodontist, plastic surgeon (yes, three times so far for facial stitching), dentist, or barbershop, it's parent-teacher night or Brownie meetings. I've come to the conclusion my wife logs more miles each year than a Mobil test driver on his cross-country run.*

*Add to this all the activities of running a home: marketing, cooking, cleaning, mopping, bandaging, laundering; and the realization sinks in that I didn't marry a mistress. I married a machine.*

*What happened to the romantic dinners and the soothing laying on of hands?*

*Where did my mistress go?*

*At least Nancie never uses that old line "Not tonight, dear. I have a headache."*

*She can't.*

*She's already asleep by eight o'clock.*

*My mistress is exhausted.*

# Kids' Lib

If we wanted to, we could eliminate the problem of step-children overnight!

Except for those who remarry after being widowed, we could eliminate ALL other stepchildren by eliminating divorce.

In *More Joy of Sex*, Dr. Alex Comfort talks about that original marriage as being the primary relationship, one that should never be severed. Its function is one of a lasting security, a permanent business agreement, and the raising of children.

Writes Dr. Comfort, "In this day of modern contraceptives, there is no reason for an unwanted child. You can plan your family, and, along with it, you accept the responsibility for raising those children to adulthood. There is nothing worse that seeing multiple-marriage people, dragging their kids behind them, with visitation rights on alternate weekends to God-knows how many ex-spouses. The children suffer badly."

Dr. Comfort also suggests that the marital boredom of that eternal relationship could well be solved by an "open marriage" system, whereby husband and wife can do their own thing with whomever or whatever they please. But the original "home" will always be there.

159

He points out that the Europeans have done this for centuries through their successions of lovers and mistresses, but *not* divorces.

Dr. Comfort, we take little comfort in your theories.

As does Dr. Robert Wald: "Fundamentally, staying together 'forever' was a good idea. The average life span of a citizen of this country used to be 28 years. You got married when you were 15 or 17, died at 28, and had a marriage of 11 years. It was sensible to stay married."

"But then we invented penicillin, and now 'forever' is such a long, long time. Now we live to be 70. So those old ideas are a hundred years behind the times. Everything is changing, right under our feet."

Sure, divorce is rough on the kids. It's rough on everybody. But what is worse: continuing a primary relationship that has two strangers living under one roof, or finding someone new whom you love and with whom you want to share a happy, fulfilling life?

**Owen:**   *I was raised in the classic tradition of the 1930s. The marriage between my parents was "arranged" by the two families. I sometimes wonder if the prospective bride and bridegroom were ever really consulted?*

*But they did marry. And they "did their duty," which was to stay married, while hating every minute of it and creating a battlefield of our home.*

*I have never seen two people so mismatched as my mother and father. But they stuck it out "for the sake of the child" and were finally divorced when I reached my twenty-first birthday. In those days, if you had to split, that was the only acceptable way to do it.*

*I sometimes wonder if they had divorced sooner, and if I had been raised in a happy home (albeit with one parent), would I myself be writing about the pitfalls of stepparenthood, the result of my own life's experiences?*

**Nancie:** *When I was thirteen, I asked my mother why she didn't divorce my father since they were so miserable living together?*

*She told me she was waiting for me to grow up, because she didn't know how she could care for me alone.*

*I begged her to leave and she finally agreed, but suggested I stay with my father for security. I said no. I'd take my chances with her.*

*We moved from the East to the Midwest where she had found a job as a fashion coordinator in a department store. She worked very hard to develop her natural abilities and became quite successful in the field. She never took a penny from my father, and she saw that I had a very good education.*

*Life was painfully lonely for me, however, as my mother was busy in her job and had to travel a lot. But I never regretted the divorce. For me, loneliness was better than fighting.*

*My greatest sorrow was that my mother never remarried. I longed for a stepfather. I longed to be part of a family.*

*And, undoubtedly, that is the reason I had children of my own.*

**Owen:** *How badly is a child's psyche affected by divorce and remarriage?*

*One morning on my radio show when we got into the subject of stepchildren, a call came in from a 13-year-old girl.*

**Caller:** My name is Tracy. I'm a stepkid. So are my two younger brothers.

**Owen:** Do you have any problems, Tracy?

**Caller:** Right now, it's pretty nice. At first, I really hated my stepdad, and I thought I'd run away from home or something. It was pretty bad.

**Owen:** Why?

**Caller:** My mom and us kids were alone for a couple of years, and then this strange man came and took my mom away. And I was mad for a long time. I felt that my mom was marrying my stepdad, but *he* was not marrying *us.*

**Owen:**  How did things finally get straightened out between you and your stepdad?

**Caller:**  I don't know how it happened. I thought my stepdad didn't like us, that we were just extra. And yet, after a couple of years, I realized that maybe he did like us after all. He had always played ball with my brothers, but one day he brought me this little stuffed green frog. And I remembered he'd been nice like that all along. I'd just never noticed it.

*Love through a stuffed green frog? Not really: "He'd been nice to us all the time. I just hadn't noticed."*

*My guest, psychiatrist Dr. Noel Morell commented: "Tracy is a very well-adjusted stepchild. Her ability to communicate is terrific. Of course she was hurt for awhile: 'He didn't marry* **us.** *He married my mom.' But see how well things have worked out! It's just a shame the new father couldn't have had the chance to develop familiarity with the kids* **before** *marriage. It could have saved Tracy those two painful years."*

**Nancie:**  *One sunny Saturday, I invited three stepkids into our backyard. One of them was ours: Peter. The other two were children of friends: Nicole, 12, and Lisa, 9. I asked them: What is it like being a stepchild?*

**Nicole:**  It's great. It's being part of a family again. And with Ted, our new stepfather, we got the best one of the pack.

**Lisa:**  Yes, it's good. Mom can stay home now. Before she got married, she had to go to work.

**Nancie:**  How do you react when Ted disciplines you?

| | |
|---|---|
| **Nicole:** | I'm kind of glad. I miss it when somebody doesn't yell at me for doing something wrong. |
| **Lisa:** | I wouldn't want my parents to let me do anything I wanted to, to say anything I wanted to. |
| **Nicole:** | We're luckier than some other stepkids. A friend of mine, whose mother has been married and divorced four times, has a new stepfather who takes a strap to the kids. They're not very happy. |
| **Nancie:** | What do you think is fair punishment? |
| **Peter:** | Being grounded. I hate it. But if I've done something wrong, it's fair. |
| **Lisa:** | The worst thing is being hit. I don't really believe in hitting someone. If you hit a kid, it's only going to hurt for a minute. But when your parents say, "Go to your room and think about it," you do think about it. |
| **Nancie:** | How do you feel when you're with your real dad? |
| **Nicole:** | It's OK. We go to the parks and beaches. But I just don't feel as comfortable as I do at home with my mom and Ted. It's just easier to be with our family. |
| **Nancie:** | Are there any disagreements in your new household? |
| **Lisa:** | Sure. Sometimes my mother and Ted argue. I don't think they'll get a divorce, but it worries me. |
| **Peter:** | When you and "O" raise your voices, I do get nervous. Because you two don't raise your voices against each other, just at us. |

**Nancie:** *What I was hearing that afternoon were kids verbalizing, adjusting to a new family environment and able to translate their feelings openly, at least as long as the ice cream and brownies held out.*

What does a pro hear from these children, after the breakup of a family and the shattering impact of a divorce?

Dr. Bob Wald replies, "I hear things like: 'I'm angry. I'm frightened. I have bad dreams.' The children often either lose their appetite or go to the other extreme and eat everything in sight. They often break up friendships with other children. Some of the younger ones suddenly form a very deep relationship with their school teacher. Others turn off to school work completely."

"Both parents and children go through a period of mourning, and at times, it's a greater sadness for the kids. They have lost the one stable experience they may have known, the family. The parents have known many couplings and have available to them the potential for making another coupling. But the children, at this point, have nothing to look forward to."

**Owen:**   *I asked Dr. Wald: "Doesn't the child realize, looking back, that it wasn't a very happy marriage? Doesn't the child remember the yelling or the fighting or the indifference? Doesn't the child think maybe it was best that this relationship be severed?"*

*The doctor's answer stunned me. He said: "The child really isn't terribly interested in that relationship at all. He is interested only in his* own *position* within *it. A child starts out with the notion that the world is his oyster. The critical issue is not whether or not his parents got along. The critical issue is him. A child sees his parents as his servants initially, there to serve him. When they break up, it comes as a great shock. He is no longer in charge of the environment around him. Now he may be a victim of that environment."*

**Owen:**   So a child is a very selfish creature?
**Dr. Wald:**   The most.

Are the problems of stepchildren showing up in our schools? Of course. Natural children have problems. Stepkids have problems. Sometimes they are the same. Sometimes they differ.

There are the Monday morning blues. A child comes back to school very sullen, having spent the weekend with his father, sailing, touring Disneyland, doing something glamorous. Then, all of a sudden, the party's over. The weekend is gone. And the child is back with plain, old mom. She becomes a drag. School becomes a drag, and everybody has a difficult week ahead.

Sometimes the children themselves are fine, but the previous spouse can cause a school some hair-raising adventures.

**Teacher Barbara Kendall:** Here's one for you. One morning a legal father showed up at school with two airplane tickets and tried to *kidnap* his own child, in a way. He told me the child was abducted from his home in Iowa and that he was taking him back right now. We're very conscious of this, the vindictive parent trying a ruse to get his child back. I would suggest that parents give the schools a statement, saying who the child can and cannot leave with. Even under this strange circumstance, we would not have let the boy go until we had checked it out with the mother.

Fortunately for us, in this case, the vindictive father was also something of a klutz. His son was not registered with us. He had the wrong school.

Yet, for every negative, we heard dozens of positives from teachers, as the stepchild from a loving home often presents less of a problem than an unwanted child from a normal household.

Teachers are readjusting their thinking, though, with regard to names. They no longer assume that the child's last name is the same as the parents'. At open houses, they are hearing: "Miss Schmidt, I'd like you to meet my mother and her friend, or, my father and his wife." In one circumstance, we were told of a child who introduced all four together to his teacher.

"I spent the weekend with my father and his girl friend" is another Monday morning sharing experience that teachers are hearing as more and more couples choose to live together.

Is this bad news?

**Psychologist Thea Lowry:** *Not necessarily. It's how it's handled. We see unmarried pairs with an assortment of children, and if everyone is comfortable with it, why not? If the children are receiving lots of love and affection from the people they're living with, whether the adults are married or not, there doesn't seem to be any problem. Marriage is a legal thing. But love and affection are the most important qualities.*

What about the legal thing? We've already gone through the tensions of divorce, the inadequacies of our court system, and the shoving around of childrens' lives from judge to judge. We've talked about visitation rights and property rights. What about childrens' rights? Who represents them? Who stands up for them? They go through a legal mumbo-jumbo, too, with no representation.

Some attorneys we know advocate that the child be represented in court by his own counsel, so that he can have more say in his parents' divorce.

Chief Judge Jean J. Jacobucci of the Family Court of Brighton, Colorado, scoffs at the idea: "I hear twenty cases a day. And there simply isn't enough time or money to appoint an independent counsel for every minor in custody cases. Most of the kids I talk to say: 'I love my mommy and my daddy, and I wish they'd get back together.' That's no help at all. A child just cannot make an adult decision."

Judge, we agree.

But still, now that we have Women's Lib and Gay Lib, might we soon be seeing Children's Lib?

Columnist Ann Landers reprinted what she calls a "Children's Bill of Rights:

1. I have the right to be my own judge and take the responsibility for my own actions.
2. I have the right to offer no reasons or excuses to justify my behavior.
3. I have the right to decide if I am obligated to report on other people's behavior.
4. I have the right to change my mind.
5. I have the right to make mistakes and be responsible for them.
6. I have the right to pick my own friends.
7. I have the right to say "I don't know."
8. I have the right to be independent of the good will of others before coping with them.
9. I have the right to say, "I don't understand."
10. I have the right to say, "I don't care."

**Owen:** *I'll buy numbers 4, 5, 6, 7, and 9.*

**Nancie:** *I'll accept them* all, *when I am no longer asked to cook, clean, wash, iron, drive, and disburse money for and to these children of supreme wisdom.*

# Courtesy, Consideration, and Compromise

A stephousehold is like a jungle. It can be exciting and lush, but there is always a subliminal fear omnipresent, that one may be sprung upon at any moment by a ferocious beast — in ex-spouse clothing. The beast may be no more serious than Bugs Bunny and the fear may ebb from time to time, but somehow it never ceases.

If marriage after divorce is worth living, then somebody has got to make the first move to break this chain of unproductive emotional reactions. Instead of regarding a former husband or wife as a slithering snake in the past's grass, how about admitting 50-50 responsibility for the marriage, the disintegration, and the divorce? And be done with it. No more blaming. Instead of savoring resentments, how about nourishing relationships?

We think it can begin with *courtesy, consideration,* and *compromise.*

*Courtesy* for the father who is supporting his children without representation.

*Courtesy* for the stepfather who is separated from his own while raising someone else's.

*Courtesy* for the mother who may be caught between her obligations to these two men, bobbing like a yo-yo.

*Courtesy* for the stepmother with her secondhand rights and silent frustrations.

*Consideration* of the children's images of their absent parent. After all, they have a right to one of each sex. For example, when a family pretends the stepparent is the biological parent in order to avoid admitting the "mistake" of a previous marriage, the children get caught in a masquerade and end up leading a double life.

*Consideration* of the time children spend in visitation; allowing them freedom to enjoy their noncustodial parent without being bombarded with the "I miss you" and "I love you" phone calls and letters, or the "guess what we have waiting for you when you get home."

When a child goes off to enjoy his noncustodial parent, one would hope the parent who has custody could adopt a hands-off policy.

A child cannot help but feel either guilt or remorse when the parent with whom he lives full time writes or phones to say how much he is missed and loved. If the child is lost in having a good vacation, he feels guilty for not missing back and, possibly, more guilt because he may equate that omission with a sign of not loving back. Under normal circumstances a child does not need to be reassured of one parent's devotion while he is visiting with the other parent. That's for summer camp, not divorce.

On the other hand if the slightest homesickness is lurking around the edges, a call or a letter like that will overwhelmingly feed its growth.

In either case you might as well kiss the day good-bye and point the child homeward spiritually. A strengthening visit gone to hell.

As for the "guess what we have for you when you get home" ploy, it is nothing less than a puerile, cheap shot.

*Consideration* for the stepparent who is not in competition with the spouse whose successor he or she is, but who does try to provide continuity and a loving atmosphere for the children.

*Consideration* for the custodial parent who faces the hour-by-hour burdens and demands of raising the children, while attempting to supply a breath of fresh air to a new mate.

*Compromise* in adjusting to the needs of the children rather than adhering to a legal ruling. Without change there is no growth so how can we be expected to live with a stilted, out-of-date piece of paper?

For instance, why should one parent be given custody of a child for his entire juvenile life? A child should be with the parent who feels more comfortable with him. Over a period of years that feeling may pass back and forth, so why can't there be flexibility in living arrangements without having to make a federal case of it?

*Compromise* in our roles. Children should benefit from re-marriages and their two sets of parents by rarely ever having to be exposed to a sitter if the families live close enough. With a little organizational planning and open dialogue between homes everybody should be able to get a change of scene without causing one.

*Compromise* in dealing with togetherness. A new step-family needs plenty of day to day contact but a new step-marriage has a right to romance. If respect for privacy cannot be instilled, install locks.

*Compromise* in our attitudes about elders. Let's not overlook that a remarriage inherits a lot of wisdom along with those additional family members. Don't we need all the help and advice we can get in "retracing our steps"? Growing up is hard work, and not only for kids.

# Best of Two
# Worlds

**Nancie:**   *I've often been asked how Owen and I have made this remarriage work, with all the personalities involved. Not only are there the six children and two middle-aged, well-developed dispositions to think about, there are also: Owen's ex-wives, their husbands, my ex-husband, his wife turned ex-wife, her children, Owen's mother and stepfather, Owen's natural father, my mother, the paternal grandparents, two cousins, and an aunt and an uncle.*

*I have attempted to extend the olive branch to them all. With most it has worked; with two it has not. I can honestly say my sleep is untroubled.*

*Perhaps there is a clue to all this in my weaknesses and my strengths.*

*My biggest weakness is my mental laziness. Coupled with my second biggest weakness, my inability to verbalize, it creates the obstacle that prevents me from handling sticky situations with finesse, and from being a truly great mother. (Are there vintage years for motherhood, like wine?)*

*Mouth-to-mouth combat is just not my forte.*

*But, if I'm well rested and Uranus is descending into my sun sign, I can rationalize any crisis: "Yes, Mummy's darling gift from heaven, I understand how you feel and I will see that your tender little psyche is not damaged while we straighten out our misunderstanding." (Do you hear me, Haim Ginott, wherever you are?)*

*Most of the time, however, I just shout and swear.*

*Chris found me out early in his life when he suggested during one of my tirades that I "go lie down."*

*I admit my attitude is all wrong. It hardly equips me for dealing with ex-family, stepfamily, new family, or blood family.*

*In fact, it's tacky.*

*On the other hand, my greatest strengths are my honesty, which I treasure as highly as the British their Crown Jewels, and my flexibility. I do not prejudge nor do I criticize. I evaluate to get insight, but I do not impose my standards on others.*

*Bending with the bamboo has kept our stepship sailing a safe and satisfying course.*

*Oh, there's one more thing, the real secret to our success, my husband, who can look at me with hot rollers in my hair and youth cream on my face and still make me a proposition I can't refuse.*

**Owen:** *It was a Sunday afternoon and I was driving Peter and two of his buddies to a super science-fiction double-bill flick.*

*Their conversation turned to their grandparents, and one of the boys mentioned that his grandmother was too old to be able to drive them anywhere.*

*Then Peter spoke, and I couldn't believe what I was hearing. "Gee, that's a shame. I'm lucky. All my grandmas drive—Nana, Grandma, Alice, and Grandma Ruth."*

*What Peter had done was group his own two natural grandmothers with my mother without labeling relationships.*

*The unit we had established four years ago had not only been fully accepted, but accepted without condition.*

*Although Peter has always maintained a close, loving rapport with his father and his relatives, he felt secure enough to embrace my family as well. I really believe that's one of the most important lessons we have taught the children—that they can love everybody without feeling guilty.*

*God knows, being a stepfather has not always been an easy job. But I often wonder if our kids aren't better off for it all. The idea of having an additional parent to care about them. Extra Grandparents. Aunts, Uncles, Cousins. Whatever.*

It may not be perfect. But what is?

**Dr. Don Lunde:**    When I talk to kids facing the remarriage of their parent, I bring out the positives. Instead of saying: "Hey, you poor soul," I'll tell them that they're actually the lucky ones and how they can learn so much from all these new experiences being offered them.

The court probation people we talked with agreed: Children of divorce today probably gain a great deal in a wholesome remarriage, and will certainly fare better than if their original parents had "stuck it out," wounding everyone in their battles.

At least in a stepfamily the children are exposed to a model of what a happy, loving couple looks like. A far more desirable act to emulate than that of the bickering parents to whom they were born. As with the Beardsley kids, they're going to realize they have a pretty good deal: "I like it here. It's the kind of home I want to have someday. And I'm going to do my share to keep it that way."

We've already recounted the story about the stepchildren, who, seeing a home full of love, actually became closer to the stepparent than the natural child of the union.

And as we've said, there are court accounts of stepparents divorcing the spouse and keeping the kids.

**Polly Bergen:**   Kathy and I see each other all the time. She calls me constantly. She is very concerned for me, and I think she's one of the best friends I have, and I'm one of the best friends she has. She called me "mother" early in our relationship although I never expected her to, and I never asked her to. And she was always conscious never to refer to me as mother in front of her natural mother. The only problem I have now is when I call her and she isn't in. I have to tell the answering service, "This is her mother from New York calling."

**Owen:**   *There's another challenge to being a stepparent. With your own kids, it's sort of live and let live, "one of these days we'll sit down and talk over things that are important to you." With stepchildren you find yourself not delaying things so much. I mean, you have taken the tremendous responsibility of being partly answerable for the lives of other human beings, human beings that were complete strangers to you, and you really feel like you want to catch up. That's one helluva challenge, believe me.*

*But the challenge pays off.*

*I can recall one particular weekend when it appeared that our house had been transformed into a Holiday Inn. I never saw so many people coming and going in my life. And most of them were not ours.*

*It all began on a Friday afternoon when Ashley had 20 of her most intimate intimates in for a swim. (I think several of them are still here.)*

*That same night Chris had a teen-age buddy in to "sleep over," a phrase I haven't been able to fully understand. Over what?*

*On Saturday morning the smell of burning bacon and the sound of crashing china reminded me that this was only the beginning. It was Peter's birthday—a new gang and new problems, including a frenzied dart game in which one of the participants nearly nailed our dog to the wall.*

*That evening, another massive sleep-in. I think the giggling and refrigerator raiding lasted until 4:00 A.M., and frankly, we didn't need that pole lamp in the playroom anyway.*

*As Nancie was making her famous Sunday morning omelette, the one with the week's leftovers in it, the phone rang. It was David who wanted to bring his friends and their new baby over for drinks and dinner.*

*"Fine," we answered, glassy-eyed.*

*"They're from Michigan and will just be here until tomorrow."*

*"Fine," we answered, glassy-eyed.*

*But, let me tell you, that night was something else. All three of Nancie's children wanted to help, wanted to make this a very special night for David.*

*Ashley, in a long dress but shoeless, became the "hors d'oeuvres" lady, passing them faster than anyone could swallow them.*

*Peter made his unique and delicious salad dressing, and set the table.*

*And Chris took a crash course in bartending, got the charcoal started in the barbeque, and prepared a strawberry shortcake from scratch.*

*All of them, giving of themselves so that their considerably older stepbrother could entertain his friends in our home.*

*And that's what it's all about, isn't it. Creating a warm, loving atmosphere where everyone gives.*

*Sure, we fight and shout and scream at each other. What family doesn't? How else can you make yourself heard?*

*But when push comes to shove there's not one of us who wouldn't stand up for our arrangement.*

**Nancie:** *This success has been felt outside the house, too. The neighborhood children pass through our doors like daily commuters at the Darien depot, to the point where we have had to disconnect the bell—not to discourage them, only to keep US from being ding-donged to death.*

*Even strange dogs wander in. Jeremy, a ten-year-old friend, made us aware of that when he knocked on the open front door to say, "Uh, excuse me. A dog you don't know just ran downstairs."*

*But there's a far more telling example of what we mean.*

*One day we were surprised to find all four children from a neighboring clan sitting in the living room. We were surprised because they had never ventured in en masse before, and because they neither wanted to play nor did they show any signs of leaving. They just seemed to want to be around us.*

*We later discovered their parents had separated the night before and in their bewilderment they had sought us out. Perhaps, because we were proof that things could, eventually, turn out all right?*

*And things have turned out all right for us.*

*How else could we feel so secure and content in this chaotic environment of ours to have been able to say: (in the middle of an argument about the outrageous number of phone calls the Anderson children receive in a twenty-four hour span).*

    **Owen:**   I want a divorce.
   **Nancie:**   Oh, that's ridiculous.
    **Owen:**   But I don't love you.
   **Nancie:**   Who expects love?

### THE END
**is not in sight**